HIS DESTINY HER PURPOSE

MATTERS OF THE HEART

Habits of a Godly Woman

TWYLIA G. REID

WHEN HEAVEN SPEAKS, LLC
WE ASPIRE TO INSPIRE

HIS DESTINY HER PURPOSE: HABITS OF A GODLY WOMAN

Published by When Heaven Speaks, LLC
P.O. Box 55
Pooler, GA 31322
www.whenheavenspeakspublishing.com

Copyright © 2022 TWYLIA G. REID

Unless otherwise indicated, scripture quotations are from the Holy Bible, King James Version (KJV), New King James Version (NKJV), New International Version (NIV), Good News Translation (GNT), and The Message (MSG).

HIS DESTINY HER PURPOSE / 1st Print Edition
Twylia G. Reid

ISBN:978-0-578-37651-6
Printed in the United States of America
First Paperback Edition

Special discounts are available on bulk quantity purchases by book clubs, associations, and special interest groups.
For details, email: info@twyliareid.com or call 912-335-3799.

AUTHORS

Barbara Johnson
Kandi Layton
Barbara Williams
Arvinese Reid
Dr. Tanya L. Moses
Dawn Cotterell
Katina Turner
Helen Newlin
Chiquita Frazier
Dr. Stacy L. Henderson
Jackqueline Easley
Sharon Rayford
Melquita Singleton
Lineshia Arrick
Dawn Pullin
Gilana Pearce
Cynthia Rucker-Collins
Evette Corbin
Dr. Anastasia Freeborn
Visionary, Twylia G. Reid

DEDICATION

I dedicate this book to our Almighty God, the Author of knowledge and wisdom...because no matter what, He loves me unconditionally!

Next, I dedicate this book to my dear sister in Christ, Shatrece Bryant-Buchanan who went home to be with the Lord 1-22-21. Trece, although you aren't physically here to let me know how proud you are, I know you are watching and smiling from Heaven. I can see you now bossing everyone around! Asking who is in charge, and if they are tracking. Lol I miss you sis. Dang Trece, what can I say.... cancer sucks!

This book is also dedicated to women around the world who possess godly habits and proudly yet humbly walk in their purpose! You go girl, keep your head high, and wear your crown with style and grace. And, no matter what, keep pouring into others until you are completely empty! I promise you, you won't regret it.

Last but certainly not least, this book is dedicated to my family. Thank you all for loving me the way you do. It helps when I really need it the most.

ACKNOWLEDGEMENT

To the amazing 19 coauthors who answered the call and said "*YES*" to becoming a part of the vision God gave me for "**HIS DESTINY HER PURPOSE.**" I am truly grateful for the journey we've embarked upon. I look forward to witnessing God's move in your lives. As the song goes, "*We are family, I got all my sisters with me!*" May God continue to bless you immensely as you walk in your purpose possessing these godly habits!

To my Friends, Readers, and fellow Kingdom Builders: Thank you for allowing the vision God has given me to uplift and inspire you to expand your everyday use of spiritual disciplines! You've made a difference in my life and I pray I made an impact in yours. I couldn't do this without you.

To my family, thank you for allowing me to be what God has called me to be in each of your lives. I know the journey hasn't been easy but To God Be The Glory!

According to Merriam-Webster, a habit is a pattern of behavior acquired by frequent repetition.

In other words…A tendency to perform a certain action or behave in a certain way!

TABLE OF CONTENTS

FOREWORD...xi

INTRODUCTION......................................xv

HIS DESTINY...xxii

A GODLY WOMAN'S PURPOSE xxiv

THE HABIT OF WORSHIP 1

Barbara Johnson

THE HABIT OF FEARING GOD 4

Barbara Johnson

THE HABIT OF HOLINESS 7

Barbara Johnson

THE HABIT OF FORGIVING OTHERS 10

Kandi Layton

THE HABIT OF SELFLESSNESS 14

Kandi Layton

THE HABIT OF PRAISE...........................18

Barbara Williams

THE HABIT OF TAMING THE TONGUE...............22

Barbara Williams

THE HABIT OF SPEAKING WORDS THAT BRING LIFE
....26

Barbara Williams

THE HABIT OF PEACE 30

Arvinese Reid

THE HABIT OF STABILITY 33

Arvinese Reid

THE HABIT OF PRAYING FOR YOUR CHILDREN 37

Arvinese Reid

THE HABIT OF SERVING OTHERS 40

Dr. Tanya L. Moses

THE HABIT OF SILENCE 43

Dr. Tanya L. Moses

THE HABIT OF GRATITUDE 46

Dr. Tanya L. Moses

THE HABIT OF MEDITATING ON GOD'S WORD 49

Dawn Cotterell

THE HABIT OF STANDING ON GOD'S PROMISES ... 52

Dawn Cotterell

THE HABIT OF FELLOWSHIP 55

Dawn Cotterell

THE HABIT OF TRUE CONFESSION 58

Katina Turner

THE HABIT OF PRACTICE 62

Katina Turner

THE HABIT OF DEPENDING ON THE HOLY SPIRIT 66

Katina Turner

THE HABIT OF WALKING IN FREEDOM **70**

Helen Newlin

THE HABIT OF COMMITMENT **74**

Helen Newlin

THE HABIT OF CONSISTENCY **77**

Helen Newlin

THE HABIT OF HOPE.......................................**81**

Chiquita Frazier

THE HABIT OF USING PRAYER AS A WEAPON **85**

Chiquita Frazier

THE HABIT OF SELF-CARE................................**89**

Chiquita Frazier

THE HABIT OF SUBMISSION.............................**93**

Dr. Stacy L. Henderson

THE HABIT OF EVANGELISM.............................**96**

Dr. Stacy L. Henderson

THE HABIT OF TRUSTING GOD **99**

Jackqueline Easley

THE HABIT OF PRAYING FOR YOUR HUSBAND....**102**

Jackqueline Easley

THE HABIT OF LETTING GO OF THE PAST..........**105**

Sharon Rayford

THE HABIT OF GIVING **109**

Sharon Rayford

THE HABIT OF RENEWING THE MIND............... 113

Sharon Rayford

THE HABIT OF WALKING IN FAITH 116

Melquita Singleton

THE HABIT OF STAYING IN THE CENTER OF GOD'S WILL 120

Melquita Singleton

THE HABIT OF FORGIVING YOURSELF 124

Lineshia Arrick

THE HABIT OF BEARING GOOD FRUIT............... 128

Lineshia Arrick

THE HABIT OF FASTING AND PRAYING 132

Dawn Pullin

THE HABIT OF SELF-CONTROL.......................... 135

Dawn Pullin

THE HABIT OF STANDING AGAINST THE ENEMY 139

Gilana Pearce

THE HABIT OF RESISTING TEMPTATION 142

Gilana Pearce

THE HABIT OF RELEASING................................ 145

Gilana Pearce

THE HABIT OF CARING..................................... 149

Cynthia Rucker-Collins

THE HABIT OF CONTENTMENT......................... 152

Cynthia Rucker-Collins

THE HABIT OF OBEYING GOD **155**
Cynthia Rucker-Collins

THE HABIT OF TAKING CONTROL OF YOUR MIND **158**
Evette Corbin

THE HABIT OF GRACE **162**
Evette Corbin

THE HABIT OF JOY **165**
Evette Corbin

THE HABIT OF RESILIENCE **168**
Dr. Anastasia Freeborn

THE HABIT OF LAYING ASIDE EVERY WEIGHT ...**172**
Dr. Anastasia Freeborn

THE HABIT OF SEEKING GOD **176**
Twylia G. Reid

THE HABIT OF LOVE...................................**180**
Twylia G. Reid

THE HABIT OF RESPONSIBILITY **184**
Twylia G. Reid

NAMES OF GOD.......................................**189**

SCRIPTURES THAT SPEAK LIFE.......................**191**

ABOUT THE AUTHORS **195**

"Your beauty should not come from outward adornment, such as elaborate hairstyles and the wearing of gold jewelry or fine clothes. Rather, it should be that of your inner self, the unfading beauty of a gentle and quiet spirit, which is of great worth in God's sight."

- 1 Peter 3:3-4

FOREWORD

By *Dr. Sylvia Traymore-Morrison,* legendary award-winning author, the only renowned African American Female Impressionist in the country, and associate writer for Saturday Night Live.

I remember meeting Twylia Reid at a book conference in Maryland several years ago. I was receiving the Lifetime Achievement Award and being recognized as the first African American Female Impressionist in the history of this country. There was a lot more to that description including being offered a contract as the first Black female writer on Saturday Night Live.

I had already written an autobiography and learned that Twylia wrote a book as well. I was intrigued when she shared with me a quick synopsis about her book entitled *Broken Wings.* I was very much aware of what it may have taken to put her story in ink, especially since it was a true story. I knew from that short introduction, I had to have a copy of her book.

Never did I realize that after reading *Broken Wings* it would change the way I looked at individuals and their caretakers who had life-changing injuries, experiences and accidents, especially those that had to do with brain damage. I never, not once in my life, addressed or knew of any one with those types of life changers.

Twylia's journey sat me down. I kept thinking to myself, this woman had to be favored. The emotions, stories and pains she described left me breathless. I could not imagine the life she had been introduced to as a result of her situation. Her book made me reflect on how often we hear about an injury of some sort and how we express our heartfelt sorrow and move on with our lives. Sure, some of us think of our friends/family who are in certain situations and some even offer to help while others can hardly deal with it emotionally. I totally understand.

Still, no matter how devastating we feel in those few moments, we have a way of moving on with our lives. Some of us offer our prayers, some of us reference it in comparison to other accidents, and again, most move on with their lives.

Twylia's courage and determination fascinated me. After finishing her book, I could not imagine how she was able to fare in life. I could only imagine that most mothers would do anything for their child. Would they in that instant? Twylia did. Her story about her and her son never left me, to this day.

Fast forward a few years. I learned that Twylia was working on a new project that would be a collaboration of several women. These women, who had each walked a path that spoke to *HIS DESTINY HER PURPOSE; HABITS OF A GODLY WOMAN!* had stories to tell about their purpose. I knew this project would be worthy of telling the world. These were women who wanted to share their walks because they each knew their story would touch many, many people and perhaps change lives. Of that I am certain. Why am I being so certain? Well, I believe it's because of their love, trust and faith in God.

While I am aware of several collaborative pieces, this "art" will surely be different. These works are from women who have lived what some of us read. Some, and I should say most, can't imagine or comprehend these types of lifestyles. However, when your faith is strong, your trust is unmatchable and you are a chosen one, anything and everything is possible. I pay attention to people like this, because being chosen is a gift in itself, at least that's what I believe.

I would like to take this opportunity to thank each person who decided to share in this collaboration. I'm sure throughout time, many people will agree and thank you from their hearts.

I believe that anyone who receives the gift of reading this collaborative piece will be inspired, led, and blessed from their heart to their soul.

You are all world worthy!

Dr. Sylvia Traymore Morrison

"She is more precious than jewels, and nothing you desire can compare with her."

- Proverbs 3:15

INTRODUCTION

The vision for this powerful book was given to me during my prayer and study time. What you spend time thinking about and doing each day ultimately forms the person you are, the things you believe, and the personality that you represent. Habits are vital for our spiritual growth. They can make or break your chances of achieving and maintaining a godly lifestyle.

Women are given the responsibility to know and defend their divine roles. Therefore, they must understand the importance of developing godly habits to assist them in carrying out these roles. A godly woman possesses great strength and is a blessing everywhere she goes. Therefore, she must wear her crown with grace and honor....at all times. And, what better way to do this than by adapting to habits that will bring about a transformation from the inside out.

Do you know your purpose? If we are to impact the lives of others and be effective witnesses, we must know what we have been purposed to do. Just as God created the sun to shine by day and the moon by night, He has created us for a specific purpose.

The world, as we once knew it, has now changed! Things aren't the same, people aren't the same, our environment and economy *are simply NOT* the same. Therefore, in order to effectively walk in your purpose, it is vital to adapt to the kind of habits that cause us to maintain positive mental attitudes and thought patterns. These types of habits will cause us to be confident in everything we say and do!

Habits come in many forms: physical, mental, and emotional. They all determine how we live our lives and how we conduct business on a daily basis. If you really just take a moment to reflect on your day-to-day routine of doing things, you could identify a lot of habits you live by. And, to your surprise, some of these habits may not be so good and you want to change them. Well, guess what, the good news is, you can! Deciding to change these habits will indeed change your life. How, you ask? Well, it's simple: when you make a commitment to change your habits, your mindset will change; when your mindset changes, your language will change; soon afterwards the way you carry yourself will change, and inevitably your life will change! Sooo, to sum it all up, when you change your habits, you will change your life.

As you cultivate a habit of practicing, your overall wellbeing will begin to improve, and your outlook on life will start to change and cause you to feel happy, inspired, motivated, and empowered. You will understand how to effectively walk in your God-given purpose and calling. When you eliminate mental obstacles, replace the negative self-talk, remove the self-doubt, and develop empowering habits, you will reap the benefits instantaneously and begin to see a shift in your life! By possessing these godly habits and incorporating them into your life daily and being consistent with your actions, you'll be taking an enormous step towards creating and building the life, future, and legacy you've always wanted.

Remember that self-kindness and thought examination are critical strategies for arousing the inherent strength you carry. At first, it may be difficult to believe but with a daily commitment to adopt these godly habits you will begin to see and have confidence that you carry strength within you.

We are often distracted from a focused purpose by daily worries and concerns. But, think about it. If God has placed a purpose before you, He will be faithful to grant you His provision to grow and advance in this purpose. But, if we are really truthful with ourselves, most times we stray from these purposeful actions because of our sinful attitudes and reactions, not measly distractions. God knows sin can deter the fulfillment of that plan, but thanks be to Him, He has also made provision for us women in the area of sin and temptation! Paul explained it best when he said, *"God is faithful, who will not allow you to be tempted beyond what you are able, but with the temptation will also make the way of escape, that you may be able to bear it"* (1 Corinthians 10:13).

GOD IS FAITHFUL! Let this truth sink deep into your bones and refresh and rejuvenate your heart...the matters of your heart that is. God will not always remove your temptations because they make your faith in Him stronger as you resist. However, as you adopt the habit of resisting temptation, the habit of self-control, the habit of fasting and prayer, and the habit of commitment, He promises to keep the temptation from becoming so strong that you can't stand up under it.

Becoming a godly woman is a process. It's not something that occurs overnight. Spiritual maturity happens in phases. Possessing godly habits will help you go from level to level, not to mention deal with the devils that accompany each new level. Focusing on the godly habits we have provided in this book will help you stay focused as you move towards becoming the godly woman you are! What better joy than experiencing the harmony and happiness, not to mention the sense of purpose, that comes with fulfilling God's plan and purpose for our lives.

We all know the Bible is a product of ancient male governing cultures. When you think about it, most of the heroes mentioned in the Bible are men, like David, Moses, Abraham, Peter, and Paul. Although this is the case, there are many amazing courageous women mentioned in the Bible as well! Great women like Sarah, Mary the mother of Jesus, Rebekah, Deborah, Ruth, Rahab, Hannah, Esther, and sooooo many more! Proverbs 31 paints the picture of the model woman and how she can make a huge difference in her home. Yes, this proverb lists the traits of a noble wife; however, they are in no way limited to those who are married. They are timeless and applicable to any woman.

God created you for a particular purpose. You...yes, you! Yes, He did. It can be difficult for us as Christian women to know our purpose. As women we are often pulled in different directions. Some of us are wives, moms, sisters, aunts, business owners, entrepreneurs, and ministry heads. There are so many voices shouting at us from different angles that can often cause us to become confused, but somehow God's Word rises grandly above the hassles with guidance we so desperately need. The funny thing about it all is that God really doesn't want much from us. He really doesn't! He doesn't come with a list of things to us as women. He only asks us to focus on the important things that will help catapult us into greatness to help us fulfill His grand purpose for those who love Him, who serve others, and who mirror Him to the world. The book of Titus in chapter two contains these ground rules for us to focus our time and energies on. These necessities, along with adopting the godly habits listed within the pages of this book, will definitely help you learn, defend, and define your role as a godly woman.

For the women reading this that already possess these godly habits, and are exercising these qualities and characteristics in their lives, and sensing God leading them in specific areas to represent Him... simply focus your time and energies on that calling! But, for those who are not, don't worry. Practice these godly habits and keep your focus on God's plan for you. Stay encouraged I tell you. As a woman reading this, you are already demonstrating purpose. You are reflecting Jesus as you live out His instructions to *"Seek first the kingdom of God"* *(Matthew 6:33)*!

To live with and walk in your God-given purpose means to focus your heart, time, energies, and main concerns on positive things that point to Him. It calls for aggressively taking advantage of each day, not only to help others, but also to prepare for future ministry. Adopting godly habits will assist you in doing so. So when opportunities of service present themselves, you'll find yourself ready, willing, and able to carry them out God-like.

HIS DESTINY HER PURPOSE is filled with heartfelt and insightful applications that will promote your communication with God to higher levels. It offers biblical sound directions and solutions to help those who may be undergoing negative experiences concerning matters of the heart. The insight that makes this work is that God fully understands! The Bible tells us in Philippians 4:6 *"Do not be anxious about anything, but in everything, by prayer and petition, with thanksgiving, present your requests to God."* Then in verse 7, it gives us a promise that if we do this then the *"peace of God, which transcends all understanding, will guard our **hearts** AND our **minds** in Christ Jesus"*!

God's plan for your life is unfolding as He leads you. I invite you to join me and the 19 awesome God-fearing, spirit-filled Christian women who have come together to share with you how to move into the dynamic that occurs when His destiny and her purpose collides!

God wants to hear from you. He longs to have an intimate relationship with you and wants nothing more than to see you happy. Deciding to make a commitment to have a better life and effectively walk in your purpose is critical to you having a positive, productive life. Once the commitment is made, the blinders will fall off, enabling you to see the opportunities that have been before you all along. Yes, that's right: the habit of commitment changes you by changing your self-identity and the way you see yourself. Once you begin to see yourself the way God sees you, you've reached the point of no return! Once this shift occurs, your entire world will change. So what are you waiting on? Let's goooooooo!!!

HIS DESTINY

Merriam-Webster's definition of destiny is something to which a person or thing is destined. It is a predetermined course of events often held to be an irresistible power or agency. Some of the common synonyms of destiny are doom, fate, lot, and portion. While all these words mean "a predetermined state or end," destiny denotes something foreordained and often suggests a great or noble course or end. The question I would like for you to ponder before you begin reading this devotional is this: Is your destiny determined, decided, discovered, desired or denied? Well, one thing we do know for sure is that destiny is never clear until you get there.

I am sure Noah didn't think that he would build a boat that would save the human race and the animal kingdom. Or, that Mary of Nazareth would know that she would fulfill the all-important role of giving birth to the world's Savior when she was just a teenager. But, they trusted God to carry them to, and through their purpose.

As we read and know the Bible today, Jesus' destiny seemed pretty clear; however, He, as a baby in the crib, didn't know He would become the Savior of the World by dying on the cross 33 years later. Possibly by the age of 12, or as Jesus continued to grow in wisdom and stature, as well as in favor with God and men, He became more and more aware of who He was and the destiny His Father in Heaven had determined. He did not have to suffer the sins of the world, He could have come down, but He didn't. This reason alone should make us grateful! He didn't come down because this was His destiny.

Destiny is not all about getting to Heaven; it's about what we do on the way. On our way to Heaven, we each have a personal destiny. We have been born and born again to fulfil a unique role in the world and kingdom of God. God is watching you, God is waiting for you to walk into and walk in your destiny. You can discover what you were designed for. Who knows, the desire of your heart may be the beginning of your destiny!

A GODLY WOMAN'S PURPOSE

What's your purpose in life? What I mean is that if you were to write down what you thought your purpose in life was, what would you say? The search for purpose in life has puzzled people since the beginning of time. Although this is the case, God created you for a purpose! Proverbs 19:21 says, *"Many are the plans in a man's heart, but it is the LORD's purpose that prevails."*

The reason that purpose in life has puzzled so many people for so long could be that too many of us have started at the wrong starting point. Think about it, when people are asked about the purpose of their life they typically ask self-centered questions like; what do I want to be? What should I do with my life? What are my dreams, my goals, and my ambitions? What steps do I need to take to be successful in life? As Christian women, we must understand that being successful and fulfilling our purpose in life are not the same thing! You can reach your goals, you can achieve your objectives; you can accomplish your aim and still miss your purpose.

It is only in a relationship with Jesus that we can discover who we are, what we are, why we are, and the real meaning, significance, and purpose of our life. Without this knowledge, we will forever wonder aimlessly in search of our purpose. God's ultimate purpose for our lives is not comfort, but character development. He wants us to grow up spiritually and become like Christ. Becoming like Christ does not mean losing our personality or becoming a mindless replica of who we already are. God created each of us all uniquely and He doesn't want to destroy that. God says we are fearfully and wonderfully made, so why would He want that to change? He doesn't! Christlikeness is all about transforming our character.

Therefore, it's important we adopt godly habits to assist us along the way. We cannot produce the character of Jesus on our own. We must allow God to work in us, and on us. You may be asking, *"How in the world can I do this? How is this going to happen for me every day?"* To be honest, it is really not that difficult. It happens through the choices we make. The habits we adopt. Choosing to do the right things regardless of the situations we find ourselves in. It's all about cooperating with God through the Holy Spirit, agreeing that His way is right, and then stepping out and beginning to do it.

Habits of a godly woman are habits designed to get you to a place where you hear from God daily as you walk in your calling. They show you directions and paths to take to effectively walk in your purpose. When you pursue something, you are intentional about incorporating it into our daily lifestyle. Use the things you are already great at doing and work on areas that need improving. This is doable by adopting great habits. Studies show it can take anywhere from 18 to 254 days for a person to form a new habit and an average of 66 days for a new behavior to become automatic. It's by doing it every day, even when you really don't want to!

Woman of God, you can do this! God will make it possible. God's plan for your life will begin to open and unfold as you allow Him to lead you. These are practices that will become great habits to transform your walk with Jesus, from something that may seem distant or stale, to something living, breathing, close, and active!

THE HABIT OF WORSHIP

Barbara Johnson

"One of those listening was a woman from the city of Thyatira named Lydia, a dealer in purple cloth. She was a worshiper of God. The Lord opened her heart to respond to Paul's message...."

- Acts 16:14-15 (NIV)

We lift our heart, body, mind, and soul as instruments that play melodies for the Almighty God. Worship is simply honoring God with our gifts, talents, and treasures. It is not limited to church buildings. Basking in His presence with the reaction of weeping, singing, or prostrate positions are simply a response to His power. Many times, we equate worship to the lyrics and the pace of songs. However, those applications can be an asset.

Communication with God is the most important way to worship. Prayer opens heaven antennas, and releases signals to God and His host of angels. Reserving space for God in everything we do produces a habit of worship.

And, when worshipping God "in spirit and in truth", we should worship expecting to have a one-on-one encounter with Him! A face-to-face with the King of Kings and Lord of Lords.

True worship is a total giving over of oneself in every aspect of our life to God. We need to approach God from the standpoint that we are in desperate need of His love, His grace, His mercy, His forgiveness, His cleansing, His restoring, His strengthening, His empowering, and His continued will in and for our lives.

Let's consider the example of Lydia, a woman mentioned in the Bible as a worshiper of God and a businesswoman. She demonstrates hospitality and seeks after God with her whole heart. Like many of us today, we are consumed with several daily tasks. Nevertheless, we can render worship wholeheartedly for His investment within us for others.

Affirmation: I will worship God and give Him thanks. He is worthy of all praise.

What do I need to surrender in order to incorporate this godly habit into my Christian walk?

_____

_____

_____

_____

What's one excuse I'm ready to stop using in order to adopt this godly habit and walk in my purpose?

_____

_____

_____

Reflections:

_____

_____

_____

_____

Prayer Focus: Ask God to help you learn how to worship Him in spirit and in truth.

THE HABIT OF FEARING GOD

Barbara Johnson

"The midwives, however, feared God and did not do what the king of Egypt had told them to do; they let the boys live..."

- *Exodus 1:17-20 (NIV)*

The fear of God is honoring His reverential position as Lord overall and King above all kings. The fear of God is not an emotional expression of being scared. The fear of God relates to a level of respect and honor. Obeying the word of God and placing Him as our priority are two main ways we fear God.

To fear God is not to be in terror, unless one is under His judgment. But for those who belong to Him, to fear God is to acknowledge His holiness, to acknowledge that He is sovereign, to acknowledge that God is not like us but is indeed the Creator of all creation! It is to be in awe of God, to be *wowed* by Him, to be unsettled and thrilled both at the same time.

When we honor God, we gain wisdom and knowledge that can only flow through His prospective. To fear God supersedes and excels over and beyond the consequences of human's ability. The rewards of our sacrifices are much more worthy.

Shiphrah and Puah were Hebrew midwives in the Bible. They were given instruction by the Egyptian king to murder all the male children, but they refused to do so. They reverenced God more than man. The fear of God empowers our faith to stand for truth and righteousness. The awesomeness of God invites us into His royal chambers. We bow in awe of His splendor and salute Him as God of the Universe.

Affirmation: I surrender my anxiety to God, knowing His peace will guard my heart and mind.

What do I need to surrender in order to incorporate this godly habit into my Christian walk?

_____

_____

_____

_____

What are some ways I can show God that I reverence Him?

_____

_____

_____

Reflections:

_____

_____

_____

_____

Prayer Focus: Ask God to help you fear Him so that you always bring Him your best, and bring glory to His name.

THE HABIT OF HOLINESS

Barbara Johnson

"Therefore, since we have these promises, dear friends, let us purify ourselves from everything that contaminates body and spirit, perfecting holiness out of reverence for God."

- 2 Corinthians 7:1 (NIV)

What is Holiness? It is a mindset of righteousness that is demonstrated in our lifestyle. God commands us to be holy. The only way to develop this habit is to accept Jesus Christ. His power through the Holy Bible can impart the ability to be comfortable, complete, and confident. Time spent studying and meditating on specific scriptures that apply to problems or situation at hand can spark flames of fire that will manifest Holiness. Holiness is a spiritual posture that is acceptable to God and allows individuals to become His instruments.

Huldah is a Prophetess of God. In Hebrew, the name

means to abide or continue. Huldah's bravery for God caused the messages from Him to be relayed to idol worshippers. She was not preaching; she was speaking the actual words of the LORD! Huldah had an important share in the great spiritual revival of the Jewish people under the reign of King Josiah, through her prophecy and influence. Her courageous acts truly displayed the habit of holiness.

The habit of holiness gives boldness to obey God without fearing man. Without holiness on earth we will never be prepared to enjoy heaven. Why? Well, because heaven is a holy place. The Lord of heaven is a holy Being. The angels are holy creatures. God is holy and so is everything about Him. Holiness is written on everything in heaven! A true holy lifestyle will only do one thing, and that's to bring glory to God. Every day, an opportunity to generate negative or positive habits is granted. The choice becomes which will it be?

In times past, the focus of Holiness has been the outward appearance but now the understanding is clear. Holiness is simply producing the fruit of the spirit, according to Galatians Chapter 5 and verse 22-23.

Affirmation: Christ has made me pure and holy!

What do I need to surrender in order to incorporate this godly habit into my Christian walk?

_____

_____

_____

_____

What are some ways I can exemplify holiness?

_____

_____

_____

Reflections:

_____

_____

_____

_____

Prayer Focus: Ask God to purify your heart, cleanse your inner thoughts and examine the very motives behind your acts and attitudes so you may remain holy in His sight.

THE HABIT OF FORGIVING OTHERS

Kandi Layton

"Get rid of all bitterness, rage and anger, brawling and slander, along with every form of malice. Be kind and compassionate to one another, forgiving each other, just as in Christ God forgave you."

- Ephesians 4:31-32 (NIV)

As I have learned and studied over the years, forgiveness is the key to having a happy heart, mind, and soul. I put most all of my worry at God's feet, as He is the One that will forgive me if I sin. Jesus is here to take upon our sins and God has forgiven us. I am one person that no matter how bad or how wrong someone has been to me God has taught me to forgive them. No matter how upset, frustrated, annoyed, or angry you are...you must forgive. Even you, if you've done something or said something you did not want to do or say you must forgive yourself also.

With a sincere heart, while you are praying to God simply

say, *"Please help me to forgive (the person's name who hurt you and mention what they did)."* Afterwards, think to yourself, would you ever want to do that to someone or yourself? If the answer is no, take this as a learning lesson on how to become a better person. Take the lessons learned from the experience and apply it to your daily life. Allow it to show you how to *not* treat others or say things to others in the manner it was done or said to you. Forgive them, and then forgive yourself!

Approximately three years ago, a man kicked me in my head, broke bones all over my body, and left me for dead on my bathroom floor. This resulted in me sustaining a traumatic brain injury. After my stay in ICU and being discharged from the hospital and rehabilitation centers, I prayed like crazy asking God to take away the anger. I was led by God to forgive this person for the senseless act he had done. It made me stronger, healthier, and equipped me with a better mindset! There is no way I could have done this without God.

What did I get in return? God gave me the strength to walk again, talk again, as well as the ability to perform daily tasks to live my best life! All because I made the decision to forgive the man that left me for dead. And, because I forgave myself for thinking negative thoughts and seeing myself as worthless while I was down and out.

One of the greatest examples of forgiving others is when Jesus forgave Mary Magdalene. Jesus could see that this woman displayed evidence of heartfelt repentance for her immoral life. And, because of this He forgave her. He told her although her sins were many, due to the love in her heart He would forgive her. Jesus did not excuse her wrong doing, but rather He manifested compassionate understanding. Forgiving others is what we must do as well. Forgiveness that comes from understanding that no one is perfect is a godly habit we all must possess.

Affirmation: Forgiveness will heal my heart, mind, and soul, and release all pain and sadness.

What do I need to surrender in order to incorporate this godly habit into my Christian walk?

_____

_____

_____

_____

Who are some of the people in my life I need to forgive?

_____

_____

_____

Reflections:

_____

_____

_____

_____

Prayer Focus: God, I pray You allow others to read this devotional and know they too can forgive. I pray that You help everyone in the world understand and feel the passion of forgiveness. In Jesus name, Amen.

THE HABIT OF SELFLESSNESS

Kandi Layton

"For though I am free from all, I have made myself a servant to all, that I might win more of them."

- *1 Corinthians 9:19 (NIV)*

Selflessness is loving other people. It is being patient and kind, it is not being envious of what other people have, and it is not being rude to other people. You may be asking, *"Why is the habit of selflessness a godly habit one must possess?"* Jesus said, "If any of you wants to be my follower, you must turn from your selfish ways, take up your cross daily, and follow me." See, it's just that simple!

Selflessness means that you love each other and give all you have no matter how little it is. We must be careful not to become more about what we get out of life than what we are supposed to give. Every day I choose to give a little bit of myself to my Broken Wings Brain Injury Group, my daughter, my father, my friends, and my pets. I do not ask for anything in exchange. My three rules in life are that everyone stays happy, healthy, and safe. God has taught me that He is love and His love is selfless. Our focus shouldn't always be on how God can meet our needs, or about what God can do in our lives. We should be focused on how we can please Him by giving to others with a cheerful heart.

In my experiences in life, I've noticed there are a lot of selfish people, people that only want what they want. People like this will not give you the time of day but yet will not think twice of asking for extras even if they don't need it. How many people do you actually know like this? I've learned that even if you just give a smile, a little wave that's considered selflessness! You know why, because you're considering other people around you by showing love that God would have shown to them. Demonstrating patience and kindness when being around others is a godly habit every women must have.

The story of Esther is a beautiful example of selflessness! She is married to an angry king when her cousin Mordecai tells her that the king's advisor wants to kill all of the Jews. She knows what she must do to stop this, also knows she can be killed for approaching the King without permission! Esther's selflessness and willingness to risk her life ends up saving her people, the Jews!

God said to love your enemies, do well by them, and lend them a helping hand and expect nothing in return. His promise to you in doing so is that your reward will be great! All you have to do is love your neighbor, and do the right things toward them and God will be pleased. How amazing is that!

Affirmation: Today, I choose to allow my needs to take a backseat to the needs of those I can help around me.

What do I need to surrender in order to incorporate this godly habit into my Christian walk?

_____

_____

_____

Write down a few things you could do that would help you be more **selfless**, and less **selfish**.

_____

_____

_____

Reflections:

_____

_____

_____

Prayer Focus: God, please put it in everyone's heart that selflessness and love are needed for the world today in these dire straits of need during COVID-19. Amen.

THE HABIT OF PRAISE

Barbara Williams

"I will extol the Lord at all times; his praise will always be on my lips."

- Psalms 34:1 (NIV)

Habit is an acquired mode of behavior that has become nearly or completely involuntary. The Webster's definition states that praise is the expression of one's gratitude and respect towards a deity. The Christian definition says praise is the joyful thanking and adoring of God, the celebration of His goodness and grace. Praise is a very powerful way to express our gratitude to God.

So many times, we tend to praise the wrong things, like our jobs, kids, husbands, our status and even our possessions; but, our praise belongs to God. We need to get into the habit of praising Him continually on a regular basis. God loves when we praise Him not only when things are going good but even when things are not going as we expect them to go. Williams Murphy sings a song

"Praise is What I Do" and there is one verse that says, *"Praise is what I do even when I'm going through."* Sometimes we are faced with situations like the death of a family member, loss of a job; this is when we should praise God even the more.

December 12th, 2019, I lost my dear mother. I watched her take her last breath in my home and the pain I felt at that moment I thought I would not get over. The Sunday after she passed, my pastor Dr. Byron Lennon preached on praise and it was as if the Spirit was speaking to me. I began to praise God and, the spirit of heaviness was lifted. I was able to make arrangements with praise. I'm not saying I didn't grieve but my praise for her life helped me. No matter what you are going through, make it a habit to praise. Let me tell you, when you praise God, something happens. Praise lifts you above the situation by helping you stay focused on God and not what you are going through. Your praise will shift the atmosphere!

Look at Mary the mother of Jesus, when she found out she was pregnant at a young age, engaged to Joseph and unmarried. She probably would think about how she would be viewed and treated by the community, but what did she do? Luke 1: 46-55 lets us know that she burst out in praise, instead of complaining or questioning.! Psalms 22:3 tells us, *"God inhabits the atmosphere of praise."*

We must develop a habit of praise. When we praise, we won't have time to complain. When we praise, we increase our faith walk. When we praise, regardless of the situation, God will work on our behalf. Woman of God, adopt the habit of praise!

Affirmation: I will praise God through all seasons of my life.

What do I need to surrender in order to incorporate this godly habit into my Christian walk?

_____

_____

_____

_____

What are some things you can praise God for? Make it a habit to give God praise every day.

_____

_____

_____

Reflections:

_____

_____

_____

_____

Prayer Focus: God help me to always have praise on my lips, no matter the situation.

THE HABIT OF TAMING THE TONGUE

Barbara Williams

"Watch your words and hold your tongue; you'll save yourself a lot of grief."

- Psalms 21:23 (MSG)

How many times have you said something and instantly regretted it? *"Oh, I wish I hadn't said that I really didn't mean it."* We tend to get into trouble when we talk too much, joke too much, and talk foolishly. The tongue is the smallest part of the body and does the most damage. Conversations filled with rumors and lies have destroyed many nations, countries, and lives. We need to make it a habit of taming our tongue.

You are being watched and a slip of the tongue will cause others to judge you based on what they see you do and especially by what they hear you say.

A couple of Sundays ago, my pastor preached and challenged us to watch what we say. I left church determined to go through the week checking my speech. Well, the very next day as I was driving my grandkids to school, a car cut me off and I yelled, *"Stupid idiot!"* My 3-year-old grandson said, *"Grandma, watch your mouth."* Right then it hit me that not controlling my tongue can influence those who hear me, especially my grandkids. Not controlling your tongue can cause irreversible damage that you might not ever be made aware of. Name calling, lying, boasting and filthy language should not come out our mouths. James 3:10 says, *"Out of the same mouth come praise and cursing. My brothers and sisters, this should not be."* When we are not careful concerning our speech, we not only affect others but corrupt ourselves as well. The scripture lets us know when we hold our tongue; we will save ourselves from a lot of grief. We might say something without thinking and pay the consequences for our swiftness in speech. We are called to be a light, and we can't be that light without taking heed to our speech.

Let's take note of Deborah in the book of Judges. She was the 4th judge mentioned in the book and the only female judge mentioned in the Bible. She was a wise woman filled with wisdom, which was clearly evident in her being a prophet of God. As a prophet, judge and military leader, Deborah had to say the right things at the appropriate time. Because of letting the Spirit lead her she rose in the ranks and pronounced sound and clear judgment. She was not loose with her tongue but conferred with God for leadership and direction.

When we speak, we always have a choice of what to say. God has given us the freedom to choose our words. James 3:8-12 lets us know that no one can tame the tongue, so our attempts to do this on our own will not work. With the Holy Spirit's guidance, this is the only way our tongue can be tamed. So, I challenge you, my sister, to watch what you say!

Affirmation: I will be swift to hear and slow to speak for the Lord has set a guard over my mouth and He keeps watch over the door of my lips.

What do I need to surrender in order to incorporate this godly habit into my Christian walk?

_____

_____

_____

_____

What can I do to prevent unwholesome talk from coming out of my mouth?

_____

_____

_____

Reflections:

_____

_____

_____

_____

Prayer Focus: Ask God to set a guard over your tongue.

THE HABIT OF SPEAKING WORDS THAT BRING LIFE

Barbara Williams

"Be gracious in your speech. The goal is to bring out the best in others in a conversation, not put them down, not cut them out."

- *Colossians 4:6 (MSG*

Remember the saying "sticks and stones may break my bones, but names will never hurt me." We know this saying is far from the truth! Broken bones will heal after a certain length of time, but words can have a long-lasting effect after the bones have healed. Many are walking around hurt and scarred from things that have been said to them in childhood from parent, teachers, and others. Some have even gone to their graves carrying the hurts spoken to them. But God wants us to speak life into people.

We need to speak life into those we meet daily. Proverbs

18:21 let us know that *"The tongue has the power of life and death..."* What we say can either destroy or encourage. Sometimes as women we are bogged down and overwhelmed, and occasionally we may lash out at our husband, children, friends, enemies or whoever crosses our path, but that should not be. God wants us to speak life into people and this is a habit that we need to cultivate on a daily basis.

Many have been hurt and a kind word from us will do them good. We need to make it a habit to speak life. You might say, how can I speak life? Well, if you see someone, render a simple compliment such as: *"your hair looks beautiful"; "your shoes are nice"; or "your smile brightens up the room."* Tell someone how much you love and appreciate them. Encourage someone. We are commanded to speak to bring out the best in others and not put them down.

A good example in the Bible is Elizabeth the mother of John. When Mary came to visit her after finding out that she was pregnant with Jesus, Elizabeth encouraged and spoke life into Mary. In a loud voice, she exclaimed: *"Blessed are you among women and blessed is the child you will bear! But why am I so favored, that the mother of my Lord should come to me?"*

Blessed is she who has believed that the Lord would fulfill His promises to her! She assured Mary that she was carrying the Lord. I'm sure these words from her cousin Elizabeth calmed Mary's fears and reassured her.

Several lives can be changed when we take the time to

speak life. Imagine you are the last person someone spoke to before something drastic happened. Did you speak to give them hope or did you add insult to cause destruction? We must pray and ask God to give us a discerning spirit and the right words to say to speak life into them. This godly habit will help others as well as yourself!

Affirmation: I can speak life into the people that cross my path.

What do I need to surrender in order to incorporate this godly habit into my Christian walk?

_____

_____

_____

_____

What do I need to do to become a life builder and not a life wrecker?

_____

_____

_____

Reflections:

_____

_____

_____

_____

Prayer Focus: God, help me to speak words of life into an individual and not be destructive with my words.

THE HABIT OF PEACE

Arvinese Reid

"And the peace of God, which surpasses all understanding, will guard your hearts and mind through Christ Jesus."

- Philippians 4:7 (NKJV)

Life is full of ups and downs, ins and outs and even some upside-down moments. Peace is seeing the facts that are presented in the situation and knowing that the God you serve can change the narrative, and if He doesn't you are alright with the outcome because you have confidence in the Author of your Destiny.

Peace is knowing you have an escape route in every circumstance. Replace worry and fear with prayer, meditation on the Word of God, and making melodies of worship unto the Lord. You are not able to right life's narrative, but you are able to establish your peace in the situation, you have control of what you allow to shake and shape your world.

We pray and give Jesus our concerns and petitions; do we rest in the peace of knowing He is more than capable and has the power to change what seems impossible to us? Rest in Him, settle your mind; there is rest for your unsettled soul. The habit of peace is rehearsing over and over the Word of God and being determined that nothing will shake your foundation of peace.

Ruth the Moabite was a great example of peace. She suffered a great loss when her husband died and left her widowed. Instead of staying despondent and unstable, she latched on to her mother-in-law. This provided a sense of peace for her. She knew who her ultimate provider was, and her future was locked down and stable in God. Be still and intentional when you pray, and soon your concerns and emotions will be washed over with the presence of peace and the sense of being whole.

You can establish the habit of peace, by not waiting until the storm hits. Make peace your daily purpose. Others will see you as a reservoir of living water and peaceful balance and ask for your recipe. Give them your best pot of Jesus by demonstrating Philippians 4:7 (New King James)..."*And the peace of God, which surpasses all understanding, will guard your hearts and mind through Christ Jesus.*"

Affirmation: I choose to look for peace and go after it. My physical man will be calm, and my spiritual man will rest in the scriptures and power of Jesus Christ, Who is my ultimate peace supplier.

What do I need to surrender in order to incorporate this godly habit into my Christian walk?

_____

_____

_____

_____

What are some ways this godly habit speaks to me?

_____

_____

_____

Reflections:

_____

_____

_____

Prayer Focus: Father in the name of Jesus, Please help me to seek You and Your peace and presence that will help me through all situations and supply me with the clarity of mind to make the right decision.

THE HABIT OF STABILITY

Arvinese Reid

"They will be like a tree planted by the water that sends out its rots by the stream. It does not fear when heat comes; its leaves are always green."

- *Jeremiah 17:8 (NIV)*

They will be like a tree planted by the water that sends out its roots by the stream. It does not fear when heat comes; its leaves are always green. It has no worries is a year of drought and never fails to bear fruit.

The heat is on! The doctor's report is not favorable, the job prospects are sketchy, the car needs repair, you name it; it's all coming at you at one time. Life's winds are blowing, and hell is boiling over in your backyard! This seems like a great day to hide your head in the sand, a great day to drop your phone in the water or send all calls to voicemail. They both equal stability and never check what they are.

Women of purpose, the Spirit of the Lord says, *"Stand firm on His Word, stand firm in His destiny."* This statement means stabilize yourself. The habit of stability is developed in the most unstable of times. In other words, your response matters, to God. The perfect time to see how firm you stand in your profession of faith, the power of Jesus that we sing about so joyfully, is to shake the earth around you. The question is not what your roots are planted in; it's how stable they are and how deep they go.

Everyone's struggle or tests may be different; you are unique. The Word that you plant in your spirit man will give you more leverage to establish the habit of not being moved, in even the toughest of times and give you influence in the places that you impact. Work, school, home, and your community are looking for stable women to help change the narrative in the lives of people.

Deborah the Prophetess and Judge knew this to be true. How did she get so confident in her call? She found that her worship brought her strength; her habit of worship strengthened her roots and stabilized her core. In the face of adversity and daily challenges of a people that were skeptical about hearing from a female judge. Deborah was used as a vessel to free people from bondage. Do people around you see you as a force to be reckoned with in stability or a leaf blown lifelessly with the wind?

The habit of stability is grown in various environments and situations. When you're met with difficulty, do you crumble, or does your green shine? The green leaves that are talked about in Jeremiah 17:8.

Affirmation: I am rooted and grounded in the Word of the Lord. I am stable in my belief that Jesus is Lord over my life and controls my destiny. I rest and hide in Him, daily.

What do I need to surrender in order to incorporate this godly habit into my Christian walk?

_____

_____

_____

_____

What are some ways I can become strategic and intentional about creating opportunities for myself?

_____

_____

_____

Reflections:

_____

_____

_____

Prayer Focus: Lord, please continue to develop in Your Word and strengthen my connection to You. Help me to be sensitive to Your presence and know that You are present in every aspect of my life.

THE HABIT OF PRAYING FOR YOUR CHILDREN

Arvinese Reid

"Don't you see that children are God's best gift? the fruit of the womb his generous legacy? Like a warrior's fistful of arrows are the children of a vigorous youth....."

- Psalm 127:3-5 (MSG)

Oh what a wonderful feeling when we receive gifts! Birthdays, promotions, holidays. And just because gifts are defined as a thing given willingly to someone without payment. Children are a gift; the scripture even says they are God's best gift.

The privilege of raising and covering God's best gift has been entrusted to you, women of purpose. A mighty task is to pray for God's will and protection concerning the fruit of the womb. You are an integral part of your children's lives. You are the bridge, spokesman, and advocate for their souls until they can reach for Jesus for themselves. You are charged by God to cry out to Him concerning your child now and beyond.

Picture a warrior who has a fistful of arrows; your prayers are the hand wrapped around the arrows; the arrows are your children. These children or any children you have charge over; natural birth, adoption, foster, godchildren, grandchildren, stepchildren, and even the neighborhood children's livelihood are dependent upon your prayers. Arrows are directed by the person holding them; launch your prayers into the ears of Jesus.

Jochebed, Moses' mother, trusted God with her son's life. She had Moses for three months (Exodus 2:1-10). This confidence she possessed that her child would be protected was developed through a habit of prayer, and relationship building with God.

The habit of praying for your children is a godly habit all women must possess. Even if you've never given birth before you are called upon to pray for children everywhere. Jesus is waiting for your fist of prayers to direct the arrows concerning His children back to Him. His instructions are simple; all He requires of you is to pray and watch the Word not return unto Him void, but accomplish what He sent it to do! Woman of God...pray for your children and for other children around the world.

Affirmation: I will develop the habit of praying for my children. The enemy's weapon may form against them, but it will not prosper. I will rise up and condemn it.

What do I need to surrender in order to incorporate this godly habit into my Christian walk?

_____

_____

_____

_____

What are some areas in life your child(ren) need prayer?

_____

_____

_____

Reflections:

_____

_____

_____

_____

Prayer Focus: Father in the Name of Jesus, help me to develop hunger for your Word, to search it and see what it says concerning my children and pray in your will, concerning their lives.

THE HABIT OF SERVING OTHERS

Dr. Tanya L. Moses

"God is not unjust; He will not forget your work and the love you have shown Him as you have helped His people and continue to help them."

- Hebrews 6:10 (NIV)

If you desire God's love and to make certain He never forgets you, then help His people. It is a blessing to give rather than to receive. The more you give, the more your blessings will overflow. One of the greatest charities is to serve others because at the same time you are serving God. The Bible tells us to support one another; pray for each other; love one another; however, it is not always easy to do. Others can cause you to be distressed, discouraged, and disappointed. For instance, Martha, the sister of Mary, showed great hospitality to Jesus and the disciples but the preparation for the visit frustrated her. Jesus reminded her focusing on a relationship with Him was more important.

We must not lose focus but seek the presence of God *daily* that you gain strength to continue serving. God will supply all your needs according to His riches in Glory. Therefore, the more you become habitual about serving God and His people, your joy will increase! Your happiness will be greater! Serving is not only goodwill to mankind and makes the world a better place, but it also aids you.

Here are five personal benefits of serving:

1. Serving brings joy to your heart.
2. Serving assists in looking beyond your problems.
3. Serving increases your sense of well-being.
4. Serving guarantees an abundance of blessings.
5. Serving expresses gratitude that can have a ripple effect, motivating others to share in assisting. Most of all, it teaches us to be selfless, not self-seeking.

Affirmation: Today, I trust myself to stay focused on God.

What do I need to surrender in order to incorporate this godly habit into my Christian walk?

_____

_____

_____

List one act of kindness you can do to pay it forward.

_____

_____

_____

Reflections:

_____

_____

_____

_____

Prayer Focus: Father, thank You for a heart to serve. Lord, please continue blessing me that I might bless others. Strengthen me to continue having the spirit of hospitality and service. Amen.

THE HABIT OF SILENCE

Dr. Tanya L. Moses

"Whoever guards his mouth, and his tongue keeps himself out of trouble."

- Proverbs 21:23 (NIV)

Parents often say, *"Listen. Stop talking because your mouth is going to cause you trouble."* They are simply specifying the importance of Proverbs 21:23: *"Whoever guards his mouth, and his tongue keeps himself out of trouble."* (NIV) Silence is the source of strength. When you are silent, it is an opportunity to be a listener and to distinctly hear God speak. It is important to practice guarding your tongue. Remember that death and life lie in the power of the tongue. Therefore, you should speak life over yourself daily.

Being quiet is powerful because it allows your thoughts to be profoundly tranquil. This alone time with God is always compelling because the clarity that you will gair from the Holy Spirit is formidable. Hannah, in her state of brokenness, is a notable example of a woman of silence. While silent she prayed about her circumstance and in God's timing He answered. There are times God is silent but never lose faith, keep trusting Him, and know His silence is to grow your faith and dependence on Him.

Just as silence is strength, it could also be a sin. It becomes a sin when Christians refuse to stand up and speak against evil and things not of God. It allows Satan to distract you. Do not participate in unfruitful deeds of darkness (Ephesian 5:11) *NIV*. When you must break your silence, let it be with purity rather than profanity. Speak wholesomely rather than selfishly. Practicing this habit helps guard your soul and keep it from troubles.

Affirmation: Today, I will guard my mouth and speak life over myself.

What do I need to surrender in order to incorporate this godly habit into my Christian walk?

_____

_____

_____

Conduct a 10-minute meditation and allow the Holy Spirit to minister to you. Afterwards, record the revelation you received.

_____

_____

_____

Reflections:

_____

_____

_____

Prayer Focus: Abba Father, please set a guard over my mouth and lips. Give me the spirit of discernment to know when to speak and when to be silent. Amen.

THE HABIT OF GRATITUDE

Dr. Tanya L. Moses

"Rejoice always, pray continually, give thanks in all circumstances; for this is God's will for you in Christ Jesus."

- 1 Thessalonians 5:16-18 (NIV)

Trials come to beset us, causing us to lose focus on God's plan for our lives. The only way to turn a trial or tragedy into triumph is to become thankful. I can remember being upset about a life-changing event that left me shattered and broken. For a time in my life, I felt unworthy. Then I decided to fall in love with Jesus! He taught me forgiveness and gratitude.

In the moments I began to thank God for my trials and tribulations, my life's circumstances started changing. I no longer carried a bowed-down head. I was able to thank God in good times and troubled times. My gratitude was rewarded. Being a habitually grateful person causes me to **"*rejoice always.*"**

Focusing on the experience of gratitude on a daily basis is how this becomes a godly habit. Taking time to truly ponder on the goodness of God and all He does for you each day will allow you to truly understand just how important possessing this godly habit is. Reflecting at the end of each day before going to bed on all the great and marvelous things God allowed you to experience can't help but overthrow you with gratitude.

Listed are Steps to Successful Gratitude:

1. Always thank God for His Son Jesus. This action acknowledges your gratitude to God for allowing His Son to die for our sins.
2. Be thankful for all the blessings He has bestowed upon you. Doing so shows appreciation to God for past and future blessings.
3. Show gratitude for the leaders in your life: spiritual, household, or at work. This gratitude will help you find it less complicated to follow good leadership.
4. Exhibit gratefulness for the family God chose for you. Having a grateful heart toward family will allow your love for family to flourish.
5. Be thankful for all the positive things that will happen in your life. This will allow positive spirits to overrule negativity.

The key benefit of living a life of gratitude is the abundant blessings that are sure to be bestowed upon you. Most of all, gratitude will give you clarity to live holy and a life pleasing to God.

Affirmation: Today will be the start of something new and powerful.

What do I need to surrender in order to incorporate this godly habit into my Christian walk?

_____

_____

_____

_____

List five things you are grateful for, and the benefit of each one.

_____

_____

_____

Reflections:

_____

_____

_____

_____

Prayer Focus: Lord, I thank You for Your mercies and blessings today. Help me to live a life of continued gratitude and to be kind and honest always. Amen.

THE HABIT OF MEDITATING ON GOD'S WORD

Dawn Cotterell

"I am your GOD. I will strengthen you and help you; I will uphold you with my righteous right hand."

- Isaiah 41:10 (NIV)

As Women of God, we must study the Bible and reflect on its significance in our lives and display "Habits of a Godly Woman." We would be depriving ourselves of a priceless gift from our Creator if we did not do so. God's Word is truly transformative, a one-of-a-kind treasure.

The powerful, biblical woman, Deborah, exemplifies strategies for accomplishing God's Will and Purpose. She was appointed by God to be a judge; a prophet who heard from God—a woman who was significant in her day. Notice how her life points to a loving God Who faithfully fulfills His promises and draws His people back to

Himself. For the good of His people, and ultimately for His glory, He transforms weakness into strength and fear into faith.

Despite being an unlikely candidate for such a calling, Deborah courageously stepped out in faith as an instrument of God's deliverance. She was indeed a woman of influence. God chose her. God *uses whomever He wants, however He wants, to accomplish His purposes.* Deborah's selection as a deliverer by God provides a model for us to surrender our lives as instruments in **God's hands.** Her life will be remembered as an example of how we can embrace God's beautiful design for us as courageous, influential Godly Women.

As a godly woman seeking to effectively walk in her purpose, I encourage you to meditate on God's Word and consider how the story of Deborah gives you true hope.

Affirmation: I will meditate on your precepts and fix my eyes on your ways.

What do I need to surrender in order to incorporate this godly habit into my Christian walk?

_____

_____

_____

_____

How will this make me better?

_____

_____

_____

Reflections:

_____

_____

_____

_____

Prayer Focus: Ask God to help you seek His kingdom above all else as you walk into the new thing He is doing in your life. Amen.

THE HABIT OF STANDING ON GOD'S PROMISES

Dawn Cotterell

"For everything written in the past was written to teach us."

- Romans 15:4 (NIV)

During my daily reading, I would meditate on scriptures that spoke to me, a situation, or a challenge that I was facing at the time. The primary scripture that I received came to me during the most difficult time in my trials and tribulations when God spoke to me in a very dream. I'd been sick, laid low with severe allergies, very weak, and attempting to deal with day-to-day issues that seemed to be attacking me from all sides.

During this time, I really don't recall saying my prayers *or* meditating on God's Word. What I do recall is God speaking to me in an audible voice, saying, "*I stretch My hand to thee; grab Me by My right hand.*" I not only heard

God talk, but I also saw His hand and reached for it. Then I heard God say to me, "*I've got you.*" Even though it was a dream, I was crying in it, and when I awoke, I was still crying because I realized God wanted me to know that no matter what I go through, He will be right there with me.

He wanted me to know that He would be my constant source of strength. God speaking to me in my weakness changed my mindset about how to not worry and to give all my cares to HIM in my daily walk.

To stand on God's promises, simply means to not give in or be persuaded to do anything contrary to His will. When you were in school you were always taught the basics. You know reading, writing, and arithmetic. Well, God's promises are the same way because they are essential equipment for our lives. They are the basics of life's lessons! Learning to stand on God's promises is a godly habit women must possess. Once you learn the fundamentals...the basics, all it will take is discipline to continue studying and learning the concepts of new material that you will have before you!

Elizabeth was unable to have children, and the community viewed this as a curse from God. No matter what others said or thought, she continually demonstrated her faithfulness to God. She believed in God's promises and gave birth to a son in her old age. Her life of faith allows us to believe that God will indeed fulfill His promises to us despite impossible circumstances!

Affirmation: I will stand on God's promises because they make me strong.

What do I need to surrender in order to incorporate this godly habit into my Christian walk?

_____

_____

_____

_____

What are some of God's promises, and what do they mean to me?

_____

_____

_____

Reflections:

_____

_____

_____

Prayer Focus: Ask God to help you understand that His word is alive and brings life to all things. Amen.

THE HABIT OF FELLOWSHIP

Dawn Cotterell

"Let us not give up the habit of meeting together, as some are doing. Instead, let us encourage each other."

- Hebrew 10:25 (NIV)

Fellowship is an essential component of our faith. Coming together to support one another is an experience that allows us to learn, grow, and demonstrate Who God is to the world. God's Word teaches us the importance of fellowship. The Lord does not intend for us to be isolated believers. He desires that we come together in worshiping Him and serving His children.

Our interactions with other believers should be uplifting, encouraging, enlightening, and consistent. In short, fellowship with other believers should be an everyday part of our lives. We demonstrate God's grace to the world. Nobody is without flaws. We all sin, but we are here on Earth to demonstrate aspects of God to those around us.

Each of us has been endowed with unique spiritual abilities. When we gather in fellowship, it's as if we're all demonstrating God. Consider it like a cake. To make a cake, you'll need flour, sugar, eggs, oil, and other ingredients. The flour will never be the eggs. None of them can make the cake on their own. Nonetheless, all those ingredients combine to make a delectable cake. It's like how fellowship works. We all show the glory of God when we combine our unique gifts.

Esther is a godly woman who exhibits this habit in the Bible. God predestined her to be queen in order for her to meet the challenge of speaking to her people. Perhaps we have come to our own kingdom to fulfill a special purpose for God through us. Esther acted in accordance with God's will in her situation, making use of every gift He bestowed upon her. We, too, must do what is right, but we must do so wisely and in accordance with our God-given abilities.

Note To Self.... I am a woman who loves God deeply and understands that communication with Him is my lifeline and a cornerstone in my life. I know that I am a better person after spending time at my Savior's feet and being filled with the joy of the Lord. I also understand that fellowship with God can take many forms, such as: bringing my burdens or hurts before Him or praising Him for provision. As a God-fearing woman, fellowship with the Lord is my lifeline. I am a woman who believes in God and understands that Scripture is my weapon against the evil one, and I will fight temptation with this truth.

Affirmation: I take comfort in belonging to God even during fellowship.

What do I need to surrender in order to incorporate this godly habit into my Christian walk?

_____

_____

_____

What are some ways to partake in godly fellowship?

_____

_____

_____

Reflections:

_____

_____

_____

Prayer Focus: Heavenly Father, I declare that every woman who loves You seek out opportunities to serve others. May she recognize that serving is not only a way for her to be the hands and feet of Jesus, but also a way for her to share her faith. Let her Ministry be important in her life because she will see the fruit it produces. In the name of Jesus, Amen.

THE HABIT OF TRUE CONFESSION

Katina Turner

"Therefore, confess your sins to each other and pray for each other so that you may be healed; the prayer of a righteous person is powerful and effective."

- James 5:16 (NIV)

It is easier to confess our sins to God than to confess our sins to one another. We can be totally transparent with all our iniquities and can take comfort in the truth of knowing we will not be judged, misunderstood, ridiculed, talked about or abandoned by Him once those sins have been confessed within the safety net of our prayers. There is no confession unbearable to the witnessing of God, so therefore I would like to be fully transparent and acknowledge the fact that I am a sinner practicing daily to walk, talk, think and be of righteous character.

Yes, I am a sinner. I don't think any of us would like to consider ourselves as sinners. *"If we claim to be without sin, we have deceived ourselves and the truth is not in us."* (1 John 1:8). Envy, greed, gluttony, laziness, lust, pride and wrath are all sins in the eyes of God. I confess that I have been guilty of them all at some point or another. I can also confess that I am still working to overcome a few of these today. Especially, regarding my unhealthy relationship with food.

God is a merciful God and does not hold us in bondage for our sins as we do each other. Many of us continue to suffer in silence and never experience true healing as it relates to a variety of experiences in our lives because it is difficult for us to be as transparent with each other as we are with God.

The Bible states that we should confess our sins to each other, while also praying for each other so that we may be healed. The story of Hagar in the Bible gives a perfect example of how a person can become the subject of someone else's envy and wrath. The type of treatment she experienced could have easily caused her to become bitter and hateful towards Sarah. I wonder if Sarah ever felt regret for how she treated Hagar.

Were they able to confide in anyone else other than God? Sometimes being open and honest about your true feelings, even if it's a little uncomfortable, can release some of the emotional baggage we carry around inside.

We must practice a habit of true confession by being able to confess our sins to one another. Knowing that we are not alone in our experiences can give us the courage to be more transparent about our transgressions. Choosing to empathize and not criticize is always good for the soul. It allows us to continue helping each other heal individually and collectively as women.

Affirmation: I choose to be committed to my own personal healing.

What do I need to surrender in order to incorporate this godly habit into my Christian walk?

_____

_____

_____

_____

What emotional baggage are you carrying as it relates to sin? Can you confess to others in the same manner you confess to God? Why or why not?

_____

_____

_____

Reflections:

_____

_____

_____

_____

Prayer Focus: God, please give me the courage to speak my truth out loud while remaining in alignment with Your Word so that I can pray with a pure heart for myself and others.

THE HABIT OF PRACTICE

Katina Turner

"What you have learned and received or heard from me, or seen in me, put into practice and the God of peace will be with you."

- Philippians 4:19 (NIV)

Over the years, I have always heard the saying *"Practice makes perfect."* I can remember being in kindergarten and learning how to trace the numbers and letters of the alphabets. The teacher would have us practice tracing each letter repeatedly until we were able to become skilled enough to recognize and write them for ourselves. I can even recall the teacher writing the word "Perfect" on my worksheet on several occasions.

This experience set the tone for the rest of my formative years. I believed if I practiced something long enough, I would become perfect at it. The two "P's" went hand in hand from my perspective. As I moved further away from the formative years of my childhood and into adulthood, my perceptive began to change. I no longer believed that practice made perfect when I failed at perfectionism.

This created some discouragement and disappointment. When discouragement sets in, depression can sometimes follow. You start to question your efforts and find yourself putting off the things you should be working to achieve. Practice no longer becomes a habit. Choosing the path of avoidance should never be an option!

Merriam-Webster definition for practice is *"to perform or work at repeatedly so that one can become proficient."* Synonyms associated with the word include **habit, method, process, and system.** We will be able to gain a renewed enthusiasm about incorporating the habit of practice into our daily lives once we understand its context in reference to scripture.

Practice will never guarantee perfection, but it can guarantee peace when you look at it from the perspective of God. "Finally, brothers and sisters, whatever is true, whatever is noble, whatever is pure, whatever is lovely, whatever is admirable- if anything is excellent or praiseworthy think about those things." (Philippians 4:8) NIV

Let's think about ourselves for a moment. We may not consider ourselves to be perfect individuals by worldly standards; however, by God's standards we are perfectly and wonderfully made in His likeness. If we develop the practice of always focusing on the Word and promises of God, and putting faith into practice, we will be able to experience His works in every fabric of our lives.

Stay persistent in your practice and keep trying just as the Canaanite women did when she encountered Jesus. She put her faith into action and refused to be turned around by His disciples. She was on a mission to witness the glory of God and in the end, she was blessed. Read Matthew 15:21-28.

Affirmation: Today, I choose peace over perfection.

What do I need to surrender in order to incorporate this godly habit into my Christian walk?

_____

_____

_____

Are you a perfectionist? Do you beat yourself up if you don't reach the bar you set for yourself? What areas of your life would you like to develop a habit of practice in?

_____

_____

_____

Reflections:

_____

_____

_____

Prayer Focus: God, You are a way maker and there is nothing I can't accomplish or overcome with You by my side. I ask that You continue speaking into my ears the words of encouragement and motivation as I continue working to improve healthy habits in my life.

THE HABIT OF DEPENDING ON THE HOLY SPIRIT

Katina Turner

"Therefore, I tell you do not worry about your life what you eat or drink or about your body what you will wear is not life more than food and the body more than clothes..."

- Matthew 6:25-27 (NIV)

"Hold on...*Holy Spirit Activate, Holy Spirit Activate, Holy Spirit Activate, Activate,* Activate. Ok, Let's go!" Does this phrase sound familiar? This catchy, upbeat, spirit-lifting phrase became a viral sensation on TikTok. Being used and seen by millions of TikTok users. Chynna Phillips Baldwin was the original creator of the phrase. I recommend listening to it if you haven't already. No worries if you're not a social media user. You can still experience this upbeat phrase by clapping your hands together, doing a little side-to-side dance and saying the phrase in unison. I just activated the Holy Spirit for myself.

I ask that the Holy Spirit be activated as I write this devotion. Let my thoughts and words be guided by Your spirit Lord. Let every stroke of my fingertips be blessed with Your anointing power so that the pressing of every key results in words inspired by You. Please remove all thoughts that are not aligned with Your Word.

How many times have we chosen to depend on and trust the words of others to validate our actions, beliefs and self-worth? Have you ever found yourself depending more on people than you do the Holy Spirit? It's ok to be candidly honest. I can recall several occasions in my life when I made the mistake of believing the word of a man over the spirit of God. When we fail to ignore the Holy Spirit, we will always end up getting the short end of the stick. We can clap our hands and stomp our feet all day long, asking the Holy Spirit to intervene on our behalf but if we are going to disregard His instruction, why ask for His guidance?

God has given us so much vision and creativity to go forth and manifest His will and purpose in our lives. In order to birth these things, we must activate the Holy Spirit to deactivate the spirit of worry, fear and the unhealthy dependency we have on someone we are not equally yoked with. Choosing to make it a habit to depend on God for all your needs will result in Him sending the right people to help you on your journey.

We must commit to immersing our mind, body, and soul into all spiritual things that awaken and strengthen our spiritual relationship with God, and being able to recognize whether we are being guided by our spiritual compass or the ego compass when it comes to developing a habit of depending on God.

Rahab displayed the perfect example of what can happen when a person chooses to depend on the Holy Spirit and to be used for His will and purpose. Hebrews 11:31

Affirmation: The Holy Spirit lives in me and guides me down the right path.

What do I need to surrender in order to incorporate this godly habit into my Christian walk?

_____

_____

_____

_____

What are some ways the Holy Spirit guides me each day?

_____

_____

_____

Reflections:

_____

_____

_____

_____

Prayer Focus: God, I ask that You be my companion throughout the day. I choose to trust in You before man. You are my provider and I will never lack anything as Your child.

THE HABIT OF WALKING IN FREEDOM

Helen Newlin

"I will walk about in freedom, for I have sought out your precepts."

- Psalms 119:45 (NIV)

What is the definition of freedom? It is the state of not having or being affected by something unpleasant, painful, or unwanted. It is the state of not being a prisoner, or a slave. The habit of walking in freedom is a very powerful one and is vital to our wellbeing spiritually and mentally.

To be truly free in Christ means the weights and bondage from past experiences are no more, and to know we don't have to accept anything that will bring us down in our mind, heart, and spirit. I had to learn that it is God's will for me to be happy, and we aren't built to carry the loads of life when He is there to relieve us from whatever it is as we move forward.

Believers today are living in bondage. Physical bondages—addictions and habits; Mental bondages—fear, depression, guilt, anger; Spiritual bondages—idolatry, witchcraft. However, you can be delivered today and walk in freedom! The habit of walking in freedom means you must never stop attacking the enemy. It is totally trusting God and recognizing the enemy's tactics in the attempt of clouding our thought patterns. We are to fight for our freedom daily, which brings peace, joy, and a positive insight of what our purpose is so we can accomplish anything we set our minds on.

To all the women reading this, young and seasoned, receive your freedom that only Christ can give, hold your head high and wear your crown with honor, and walk in your purpose boldly. Don't settle to be taken back, but press forward and watch God do great things in your life. Woman of God, you are FREE!

Mary Magdalene displayed this godly habit after encountering Jesus. She was in the act of the bondage of adultery. The accusers that brought her to Jesus said she was to be stoned as their law mentioned. Jesus said to the crowd, *"For anyone without sin to cast the first stone."* This resulted in everyone present turning and walking away. He asked her where her accusers were, and she replied she didn't see any. He then said the same and told her, *"Go, and sin no more!"*

How liberating she must have felt to know that all the heaviness of her sins was forgiven! She didn't have to hold her head down in shame anymore, and had a new freedom in Christ! She continued on with Jesus as one of His devout followers and disciple.

The same for us, with knowing we are free in Him. We can continue on unashamed, head held high, and with boldness, no more bondage, or chains but freedom. That is great news!

Affirmation: Freedom is a choice, and I am empowered to do great things through Christ Who strengthens me.

What do I need to surrender in order to incorporate this godly habit into my Christian walk?

_____

_____

_____

_____

What's one lie I'm ready to stop believing about myself so that I can walk in my purpose?

_____

_____

_____

Reflections:

_____

_____

_____

_____

Prayer Focus: Lord, I thank You so much for loving me into my freedom in You. I thank You that by Your guidance, love and care, chains are broken so I can continually see myself as You see me.

THE HABIT OF COMMITMENT

Helen Newlin

"Let us not become weary in doing good, for at the proper time we will reap a harvest if we do not give up."

- Galatians 6:9 (NIV)

What is the definition of commitment? It is an attitude of someone who works very hard to do or support something. When I think of commitment, it is not just an attitude, but a sincere focus of a mature mindset as well. Many times, this habit is taken for granted, meaning the thought can come to our minds to say, *"Why should I do it all when I see others aren't putting in the effort?"*

Before accepting any task, whether from your employer in volunteering to do a project, from family, in rotating between them in taking care of a sick relative, or from leadership in your ministry, ask yourself, *"Am I willing to do it wholeheartedly, and go the extra mile if need be? Do*

I understand that my full or lack of commitment will affect others involved for the positive, or the negative?" It is also very important to be willing to receive instructions from the ones that asked for your assistance so things will function properly.

God sees our commitment even if others may not, so don't give up or quit, my sister; your reward is coming from serving with a pure heart.

Ruth displayed this godly habit by showing her commitment to her mother-in-law Naomi, and it showed how God has called us to be committed to Him, and to one another. Ruth told Naomi, *"Where you go I will go, where you lodge I will lodge your people shall be my people and your God my God where you die I will die and there will I be buried."*

These are words of love. Love is best defined as commitment. And in Ruth's comments to Naomi we see the two most important parts of Christian love or commitment. Commitment to God and commitment to one another!

Affirmation: I will commit to making things better, no matter what situation I am in.

What do I need to surrender in order to incorporate this godly habit into my Christian walk?

_____

_____

_____

_____

What is the one revelation God showed me after reading this content?

_____

_____

_____

Reflections:

_____

_____

_____

Prayer Focus: Lord, help me to understand that my commitment is displaying my loyalty to You. Even if others may think otherwise, it is pleasing in Your sight with the work of my hands. Keep my mind focused on You as I go about my daily assignments.

THE HABIT OF CONSISTENCY

Helen Newlin

"Therefore, my dear brothers and sisters, stand firm. Let nothing move you. Always give yourselves fully to the work of the Lord, because you know that your labor in the Lord is not in vain."

- 1 Corinthians 15:58 (NIV)

What is the definition of consistency? It is the quality or fact of staying the same at different times. When I think of this habit, I visualize it as a driving force to go when others tend to give up, or fall off. I personally live this daily, and I must stay close to God because it comes with a cost. What does that mean? It is a settled decision to carry out what is to be done on purpose, but with passion in what I do.

Consistency is also repetitive, and requires more of us as we move from one level to another, and if we're not careful, we can get caught up in the business of it to say, *"Is this worth it? I don't see anything happening for me yet."* When that happens, it is good to step back for a moment, breathe and talk to God. We are to be reminded that He is with us through those times, and the diligence of it will pay off for our good.

I'm thankful for my Pastor in reminding us of this. I'm one of the leaders in music ministry with our praise and worship team and choir. He mentioned not only to be mindful of the enemy's tricks to try to come in to cause complacency, but to continue to be on the "cutting edge" in excellence in the kingdom of God. That shook me! Regardless of how long I've been doing it, I must stay humble and never forget it's not about me, but for someone else's deliverance.

Consistency is a wonderful habit to use as one seeking to effectively walk in her purpose. If we continue in it, we will reach our destination. Spiritual consistency is a magnificent outcome of a well-developed spiritual life. Neglected spirituality naturally tends to stagnancy then gradually falls into spiritual deterioration. Spiritual nourishment and the right association are very essential to every believer. Obedience to the Word of God is a great door to spiritual consistency.

Miriam, Moses' sister, portrayed this godly habit. She and her mother hid her brother for 3 months because of a decree from Pharaoh. He ordered for all Hebrew boys to be killed by casting them in the Nile River. In that, they placed him in a basket, and placed him in the banks of the river, and Miriam watched closely, never leaving his side.

When Pharaoh's daughter discovered him, Miriam quickly asked if a Hebrew woman could nurse the child which would be her mother. The Princess said yes, and commanded them to bring him back when he was older; that saved her brother's life! This example showed an unstoppable consistency by Miriam to have a positive outcome for Moses.

Affirmation: I will develop the habit of consistency and trust God to do all He has promised to do for me.

What do I need to surrender in order to incorporate this godly habit into my Christian walk?

_____

_____

_____

_____

What are some areas I am not consistent in that I need to change in order to walk in my purpose?

_____

_____

_____

Reflections:

_____

_____

_____

_____

Prayer Focus: Lord, I thank You for insight to put off procrastination. I'm happy to know that by talking to you, I regain my focus and strength to finish what is set before me.

THE HABIT OF HOPE

Chiquita Frazier

"May the God of hope fill you with all joy and peace as you trust in him, so that you may overflow with hope by the power of the Holy Spirit."

- Romans 15:13 (NIV)

Are you living without hope? Do you think your condition is just hopeless? Hope is not just wishing but it is an outright expectancy. It is choosing to look for and expect positive outcomes, even during situations where there seem to be no way out.

Have you ever really asked yourself why having hope is so important in life? Well, I asked myself this in March of 2021 when I discovered I had breast cancer. I remember when I got the phone call at work from my doctor informing me I had cancer. With unstoppable tears crying out to God, I felt empty and lost. My body was so weak. I remember telling God I needed Him like never before.

I then called my daddy, my Pastor, who immediately began praying with me and for me as we petitioned our Heavenly Father, our God of Hope. Three things came to mind: how was I going to tell my children, what was I going to do, and why me? Then the Holy Spirit softly said *"Why not you?"* 2 Timothy 1:7 says *"For God hath not given us the spirit of fear; but of power, and of love, and of a sound mind."* I knew then God was moving on my behalf. Why, because God's Word gives us hope!

In life, we go through things and think nothing of it but God told me this was something I had to endure. Within three months of this journey, with God by my side, I had three surgeries and many different tests. Starting one of the strongest chemo drugs on the market called the "red devil" I told the nurse my name for it was the *blood of Jesus.* After my first treatment I felt I could do this. My weekend was good, but then came Monday. I woke up to the worst pain ever. Crying and afraid, I began to cry out to God like never before. At this point, I knew I was really sick...but God!

Just like the woman with the issue of blood who touched the hem of Jesus' clothes. She was in a hopeless situation. She not only had hope but faith. Her hope was unordinary hope. She had hope because she knew Who Jesus was. And, just like this woman, I too had hope because I knew He was with me.

Hope is to believe, desire, and trust. I learned not to trust in my prayers but trust in the One who can answer my prayers. Hebrews 11:1 states that *"Now faith is the assurance of things hoped for, the conviction of things not seen."* Hope leads to faith! This is why the habit of hope is so important in life.

Affirmation: I will develop the habit of praying for my children. The enemy's weapon may form against them, but it will not prosper, I will rise up and condemn it.

What do I need to surrender in order to incorporate this godly habit into my Christian walk?

_____

_____

_____

What hopeless situation do you need to give to God?

_____

_____

_____

Reflections:

_____

_____

_____

Prayer Focus: Ask God to touch you, and fill you with His light and His hope.

THE HABIT OF USING PRAYER AS A WEAPON

Chiquita Frazier

"For we wrestle not against flesh and blood, but against principalities, against powers, against the rulers of the darkness of this world, against spiritual wickedness in high places."

- Ephesians 6:12 (KJV)

Using prayer as a weapon is a godly habit we all need to possess. As Christian women, we need to really see what God says about prayer and find its biblical view that we should have in order to effectively walk in our purpose. The definition of the word weapon is an instrument or device used to cause bodily harm. Prayer is "talking to God." Prayer is not meditation or passive reflection; it is just simply talking to God. What a beautiful thing!

I remember sitting staring at the stars as a young lady with two kids at the time learning I was yet again pregnant with my third child at the age of 20. I felt it was too much for someone my age to bear. The thought of dealing with bad relationships, bills, children, and so much more was all overwhelming. I felt like I was fighting demons in the natural! Suddenly, I remembered a young lady once spoke to me and said, *"God will meet you in His Word."* At that moment I remembered, the weapons of life can't cause me bodily harm or destroy me.

John 10:10 states, *"The thief comes only to steal and kill and destroy. I came that they may have life and have it abundantly."* God's message to us is, *"Do not be afraid or discouraged because of this vast army. For the battle is not yours, but God's!"* God called the body of Christ to be more than conquerors, to tread upon snakes and scorpions, and to storm the gates of hell and to wreak the same havoc that Jesus and Paul did individually. Using prayer as a weapon allows us to become strong in the Lord, and in the power of His might.

The weapon of prayer versus the natural weapons in your life is more powerful, unstoppable, and deadlier than you can ever imagine. We must put on the full armor of God, so we may be able to stand against the tricks of the devil.

We have a calling to pray because without prayer we have no strength. Female prayer warriors in the Bible are seen throughout Old and New Testament scriptures. Hannah, the Prophet Samuel's mother, knew how to use prayer as a weapon. She would go to the temple and pray daily to God for a child. She promised God if He blessed her with a child she would give him back to Him. God answered

Hannah's prayer by giving her not just one child but seven!

We should see God's grace in everything. Women of God, learn how to be grateful for the good and the bad as you use prayer as your ultimate weapon!

Affirmation: No weapon formed against me shall prosper because I am more than I am more than conqueror through Christ who strengthens me.

What do I need to surrender in order to incorporate this godly habit into my Christian walk?

_____

_____

_____

What are some areas in your life where prayer has been a weapon?

_____

_____

_____

Reflections:

_____

_____

_____

Prayer Focus: Ask God to create in you a clean heart that you may be worthy of Him. Ask Him to teach you how to use prayer as a weapon as you face things that are unlike Him.

THE HABIT OF SELF-CARE

Chiquita Frazier

"Therefore, I urge you, brothers and sisters, in view of God's mercy, to offer your bodies as a living sacrifice, holy and pleasing to God—this is your true and proper worship."

- Romans 12:1 (NIV)

Women, we are different in many ways. We come in different shapes and sizes, different shades of color, and different cultures. This is what makes us so unique. We are all beautiful! The word "habit" means a settled or regular tendency or practice, especially one that is hard to give up.

The habit of self-care is very important to all women. Self-care is more than what you may see. It is vital for women to possess this habit to be effective in all they do. It is important to God that we take care of ourselves. We have habits of letting people tear us down just to build themselves up. We are called all kinds of things: fat, unworthy, not smart enough, you will never amount to anything, and the list goes on. Mark 12:31 says, *"'Love your neighbor as yourself.' There is no commandment greater than these."* This is proof that God not only approves of us practicing self-care, but also He *commands* it! How can we love anything or anyone if we can't or don't know how to love self? The truth is, we really can't.

Self–care begins with God and ends with Him. Jesus even displayed self–care when He separated Himself from the others to pray, when He rested, and even when He meditated on God's word each day.

So getting the right amount of sleep, exercising, maintaining a healthy prayer life, and getting away from learned negative behaviors are some examples of self-care. With all of this being said, we need to adapt the I A.M.'s of Life: *I am the apple of God's eye; I'm more than a conqueror; I am the head and not the tail; and I am a rare diamond.*

Proverb 31:30-31tells us, *"Charm can fool you, and beauty can trick you, but a woman who respects the Lord should be praised. Give her the reward she has earned; she should be praised in public for what she has done."* We need to take care of ourselves. We bear the image of God, and it brings Him glory when we take care of the body He's given us. Practice self-care for your soul as well by reading God's word, spending time in prayer, and fellowshipping with others.

Wake up, woman of God, and know who you are. Cherish the vessel you have. You are the righteousness of God in Christ Jesus, and real life, abundant life does indeed belong to you!

Affirmation: I will take care of myself so I can take better care of others.

What do I need to surrender in order to incorporate this godly habit into my Christian walk?

_____

_____

_____

What are some ways to practice self-care?

_____

_____

_____

Reflections:

_____

_____

_____

Prayer Focus: Ask God to allow you to enjoy good health so all may go well with you in your physical body, even as your soul is getting along well.

THE HABIT OF SUBMISSION

Dr. Stacy L. Henderson

"Submit yourselves therefore to God. Resist the devil, and he will flee from you. Draw nigh to God, and he will draw nigh to you..."

- James 4:7-10 (KJV)

Being submissive is more than just conforming to the will or authority of another; it involves intentional acts of surrender on our part. That is what God expects of us; repentance of our sins, acceptance of Jesus as our Lord and Savior and allowing Him to reign in our lives. These are essential components of submission - which ultimately renders unto us salvation. When one totally submits to God, their all is given to His will and purpose for their lives.

As Christians, when we submit to God, we must freely give our lives to Him. This is an affirmation of our faith and a promise to do His will. Submission requires a shift in our way of thinking; our mind should be focused on God. His grace is sufficient for us (2 Corinthians 12:9). Therefore, we must rely on Him for everything and trust in all that we do.

Submission is a good habit to develop in order to live a life of freedom. When our steps are ordered in the Word of God and according to His will, we are set on a course that directs us along the path of righteousness. When we walk with godly purpose and heed the voice of the Lord, we experience an abundance of endless blessings (Deuteronomy 1:2).

We must humble ourselves and practice humility in our dealings with one another, while allowing God to exalt us in His way and in His time (1 Peter 5:5-7). Although godly submission is essential, submission to those in authority over us is also necessary. For example, relationships between parents and children (Ephesians 6:1-3); husbands and wives (Colossians 3:18-24); and those in leadership positions of authority (Hebrews 13:17) require us to submit to the will of authority. In doing so, we honor God by exercising a submissive will which is the standard that He has set for us (1 Peter 2:13-14).

Affirmation: I will submit to God and in all ways honor Him with my life.

What do I need to surrender in order to incorporate this godly habit into my Christian walk?

After adopting this godly habit, how can I use what I am already good at to help me walk in my purpose?

Reflections:

Prayer Focus: Ask God what you must do to fully submit to Him. Then, affirm your commitment by yielding to His will and purpose for your life.

THE HABIT OF EVANGELISM

Dr. Stacy L. Henderson

"And many of the Samaritans of that city believed in Him because of the word of the woman who testified, "He told me all that I ever did..."

- John 4:39-41 (NKJV)

Evangelizing is bearing witness to the goodness of the Lord. By doing so, the teachings of the Gospel of Jesus Christ are shared with others through our words and our actions. Christians are expected to be shining examples of Christlikeness. When it comes to evangelizing, the Woman at the Well is one of the first persons that come to mind. She met Jesus in an unlikely place; a location that Jews avoided so they would not encounter people of her lowly status. And just like her, Jesus meets us where we are.

Surely, the woman was surprised when Jesus spoke to her, because normally Jews and Samaritans did not have anything to do with each other. The two of them engaged one another in conversation, which led her to develop a belief in Him. So much so that she wanted others to know about Him. So, she took the initiative and set out to share her experience with the people of her hometown. She gave great witness when she returned to tell everyone of her life-changing encounter with Jesus at the well.

It is imperative that we develop the habit of evangelizing; sharing our experiences with God, so that others want to encounter Him also. We must not be ashamed of the Gospel of Jesus Christ and go forth, telling others of His goodness. Society often shuns us based on our troubled pasts or misdeeds; however, Jesus has a very different perspective. Just like He viewed the Woman at the Well, Jesus sees us through the eyes of God: He gazes on us with unconditional love. He showers us with His blessings - not because of who *we* are BUT because of Who *He* is. He looks beyond our faults and meets our needs. Whereas society rejects us for trivial reasons, Jesus loves!

Affirmation: I will unashamedly bear witness to God's goodness, grace and mercy.

What do I need to surrender in order to incorporate this godly habit into my Christian walk?

What are some ways I can evangelize to others and share the goodness of the Lord?

Reflections:

Prayer Focus: Affirm your commitment to God by sharing the Good News of the Gospel of Jesus Christ through your spirit-filled worship, your good works and your unapologetic witness.

THE HABIT OF TRUSTING GOD

Jackqueline Easley

"Trust God from the bottom of your heart don't try to figure out everything on your own. Listen for God's voice in everything you do..."

- Proverbs 3; 5-6 (NIV)

Trusting God is imperative to our Christian walk, and allowing God to see that you trust Him in everything you do is a way to strengthen your covenant with HIM! To trust something or someone means: "A firm belief in the reliability, truth, ability, or strength of someone or something" (www.merriam-webster.com).

Many can trust God for the big things, but most times we have difficulty trusting Him for the things or people we hold close to us. Things like our money, our relationships, our faults, or sickness. The habit of trusting God is one that many will not master because it takes giving up your will in Him and allowing HIM to take complete control of every part of your being.

As I speak to the women who will be reading this devotional, if you are anything like me, you want complete control over the things and people you hold dear, but I had to empty out all of my own selfishness in order to trust God and not try to figure out or know what the end would be. All I knew is that if I would listen to the voice of God in every situation, then He would make sure I stayed on track and the end result would be perfectly ordained by Him.

If I can engage your thinking for a second, I will like to share one of my past life experiences. Many years ago, as a young woman, I was divorced and faced to raise 3 kids alone. At the time I was making very little in income and I struggled to make a life fitting for my kids. I wanted to return to school to obtain my nursing degree, but didn't have the means or funds. I began to take my prayer life more seriously. I asked God what I could do to trust Him more, even when I didn't see the resources. I had to learn to be one with the Lord and trust His plan, not mine. As I began to trust His plan in my life, He not only sent resources for me to finish school, but also made a way for me to care for my children.

The Bible shows us a wise woman who was God-fearing name Jochebed, who had to save her child from Pharaoh. She hid her son and then placed him in a basket in the Nile River to save his life. This woman did not know what would happen, but she trusted God to keep her son safe and to allow him to drift to a safe place.

Affirmation: I must trust God, when I can't see the end.

What do I need to surrender in order to incorporate this godly habit into my Christian walk?

_____

_____

_____

_____

What do I need to do to trust God, when I can't see His plan in my life?

_____

_____

_____

Reflections:

_____

_____

_____

_____

Prayer Focus: Ask God to help you let go of your will and cling to His will, Amen.

THE HABIT OF PRAYING FOR YOUR HUSBAND

Jackqueline Easley

"Though one may be overpowered, two can defend themselves. A cord of three strands is not quickly broken."

- Ecclesiastes 4:12 (NIV)

Marriages are being attacked and the divorce rate is extremely high. Being a godly woman, I am led to challenge wives who read this devotional to develop a godly habit of praying for their husbands and families. When we develop a habit of praying without ceasing for our spouses, we summon God into our marriages, finances, business ventures, and everything concerning our marriages. We must commit ourselves into a life of prayer and worship with God, and we must remember the enemy is trying to destroy marriages. As women of *prayer*, we must declare in the earth that we will stand to defend our husbands in prayer.

In June of 2019, in the midst of COVID, my husband became sick with this horrible sickness. I can remember being at work and getting a text message from him that he was so sick he could not get out the bed. Initially I was afraid, because this disease had already taken so many of our friends, but I heard the voice of God speak to me and instruct me to begin to pray throughout my home 4 times a day for my husband's health. God was teaching me to develop a habit of prayer for my husband! I always prayed for my husband, but at this time I had to be specific in my prayer and I followed the instructions of the Lord. As I began to move through the rooms in my home and anoint my husband's body, the Lord was healing him with no residual effects from COVID.

The Bible speaks of a woman name Priscilla who was married to Aquila. They had a ministry for the Lord. They loved God and the church, and their marriage exemplified prayer and love. Priscilla had to be a woman who developed a habit of prayer for her husband to endure the attacks of the enemy and to work in ministry. My husband and I are Pastors, and the enemy will always try to destroy your home when you are committed to the work and ministry of the Lord. God strengthened my habit of prayer for my husband during his sickness. To God be the glory!

Affirmation: I will pray without ceasing for my husband.

What do I need to surrender in order to incorporate this godly habit into my Christian walk?

_____

_____

_____

_____

What's the first step I need to take to adopt this godly habit to effectively walk in my purpose? What is the one revelation God shared with me after reading this content?

_____

_____

_____

Reflections:

_____

_____

_____

_____

Prayer Focus: Ask God to teach you how to develop the habit of praying for your husband.

THE HABIT OF LETTING GO OF THE PAST

Sharon Rayford

"And we know that all things work together for the good of those who love God, to them who are called according to his purpose."

- Romans 8:28 (KJV)

Letting go is a releasing or separating of oneself from something or someone. It is forgiving, suffering, welcoming, and so forth. In life daily choices consist of evaluating ourselves and then deciding what should remain or not. Letting go is not always an easy task, but a necessary action of the heart. Making the right choice, God must be in the midst in order to gain courage and strength to follow through.

There are many habits that many may form in various areas, but the habit of letting go of the past is usually not at the top of the to-do list. Growing in God, forgiving others of past wrongs, forgiving yourself, welcoming change, and suffering all work together for the good. Trials and tribulations will come. Be encouraged, your labor is not in vain. Those that are mothers know the feeling of letting go. The child grows up and heads off to college and another graduates high school or gets married. The relationship is still there, but the position has shifted from seeing them on a daily basis to receiving a phone call or text every other day.

Let us talk about the measures a woman took to let go of someone dear to her. In Exodus 1 - 2 (KJV), Joseph died and Pharaoh the new king of Egypt commanded the midwives to kill all the male babies of the Hebrew women by drowning them in the river. Can one picture watching a mother's child being drowned right in front of you! Oh the screams of pain and anguish!

Jochebed, a Hebrew woman, had a son later named Moses. She was in the midst of this horrific situation and needed God to intervene. Killing her son was never an option. Time passed, and a decision had to be made. She concealed him in a water-proof basket and placed him in the river. Later, her son was found and she was hired to nurse her own child!

Let's take a look at this story in a different way. Imagine that the midwives killed the babies instead of fearing God. Think about those that have had an abortion, or those that have a past full of regrets. God searches the heart and loves us all. He loves us so much that He gave His only Son to die, to shed His precious blood so that all can be free and receive a more abundant life. Regardless of the past, let it go, give it to God. Move from fear to faith.

Affirmation: I am letting go of my past, so I can have a brighter future.

What do I need to surrender in order to incorporate this godly habit into my Christian walk?

_____

_____

_____

What am I showing God by holding on and not letting go of the past? Is there anything in my past I believe is worth not letting go of?

_____

_____

_____

Reflections:

_____

_____

_____

Prayer Focus: Lord, help me to let go and allow you to have full reign in my life. Amen

THE HABIT OF GIVING

Sharon Rayford

"Therefore I have lent him to the Lord: as long as he lives, he is given to the Lord."

- ***1 Samuel 1:28 (KJV)***

Giving is a seed sometimes covered, but grows into a beautiful flower. This seed must be released from within to a holy God to give the increase. This flower is nourished in love. Its stem is also a warm hug, comfort, handing someone thirsty a cool glass of water, and many times sacrifices. Giving is granting opportunities to others, committing without asking, releasing what has been planted within, and obedience to God. This is an act of faith from the heart to our loving God, the Father of giving.

A habit is becoming rooted in a particular way of life from much practice. It does not happen overnight, but with persistent effort and humility to God habits will form. As we embark on the godly habit of giving, let us be Spirit-led and not operate in mere routine. In areas of weakness, God never stops giving us His wonderful love.

Giving is an attribute of God. He gave the ultimate sacrifice, His Son, Christ Jesus. It is a beautiful expression of love and importance in our Christian walk. Keep in mind that the Word of God tells us to purpose in our *own* hearts what to give, but not with a grudge, 2 Corinthians 9:7 (KJV). Giving is a matter of the heart. Whatever is in our hearts will show.

Let us take a look at Hannah, a barren Jewish woman, heartbroken and shunned. She threw all cares upon the shoulders of her mighty God. She held up her shield of faith as the darts came. Her actions replicated the love of God by releasing what was precious to her, a son. God broke the chains off of Hannah's life by opening her womb. Her sadness now became joy. Her bondage now liberty. She had now become fertile ground. She did not become weary of well-doing. Her hope was not in vain. Reaping was around the corner.

Hannah truly possessed the habit of giving. Can one imagine the challenges she faced? She still pleased God; for her desires were faith-led not pressure-led. Hannah did not make excuses. She purposed in her heart to pray instead. She did not use choice words with Peninnah, her husband's mother that was ridiculed by her. God saw the heart of Hannah; He not only gave her a son, but also overflowed her with restoration. Because she gave, God changed her story. He heard her cry and fulfilled her plea!

God placed on her table love that conquers all, more abundant life, and peace because her mind stayed on Him. He is a Giver and none can beat God in doing so.

Affirmation: I am purposing in my heart, by faith, to worship God in giving.

What do I need to surrender in order to incorporate this godly habit into my Christian walk?

_____

_____

_____

_____

In what ways do I give to God in the midst of tribulation?

_____

_____

_____

Reflections:

_____

_____

_____

_____

Prayer Focus: Ask God to heal all hurt or pain that hinders giving in love. Amen

THE HABIT OF RENEWING THE MIND

Sharon Rayford

"And Ruth said, Intreat me not to leave thee, or to return from following after thee: for whither thou goest, I will go: and where thou lodgest, I will lodge: thy people shall be my people, and thy God my God."

- *Ruth 1:16, 17 (KJV)*

"The mind is a terrible thing to waste" is a common saying. It is truly important and God speaks about the mind throughout His word. The mind must be bathed from unclean thoughts in order to make good decisions, and ultimately channel our thoughts on the things of God. A sound mind is our portion!

To renew is to rebuild, repair, make new, to renovate. To begin again is allowing the word of God to change the desires of the heart to those that please Him. The former things are not things that bring pleasure to our Holy God, but cost the ultimate sacrifice in order to have an opportunity to walk in newness. Renewing the mind is how we can truly become effective in this walk. Forming a habit that shifts from old to new is one that requires consistent dedication to God. Often times, it is pressing to move from our place of comfort. However, the ways of old, the past, or giving over to the flesh is a habit we have been given power to break, Luke 10:19 (KJV).

The habit of renewing the mind is the action of seeking and obeying God. God offers the believer spiritual renewal from a carnal mind to the mind of Christ. Renewing the mind is an intentional surrendering to the Spirit of God, by repenting of convicted sins. When things come up that are not of the new man, we must cast it away from us and hold on to God's love.

There will be situations that arise in life that forces us to examine the present condition. That decision will bring about a change in direction. If Ruth was here today, she could expound on the subject matter. Her name means "grace." Coming from Bethlehem to Moab, she remained by the side of her mother-in-law mourning her two sons. Ruth changed her mind and her god from Chemosh to the Almighty when she married Boaz.

Ruth experienced the favor of God when she obtained a "made-up mind." She stepped out of the old and into a whole new life of blessing, love, and servitude. Possessing this godly habit is indeed vital for you to effectively walk in your purpose.

Affirmation: As I walk in newness with Christ beside me, my mind will change.

What do I need to surrender in order to incorporate this godly habit into my Christian walk?

_____

_____

_____

_____

In what areas of my life do I observe a renewed mind?

_____

_____

_____

Reflections:

_____

_____

_____

_____

Prayer Focus: Ask God to renew your mind and keep your focus sharp as you pursue His purpose for your life.

THE HABIT OF WALKING IN FAITH

Melquita Singleton

"For we live by faith, not by sight."

- 2 Corinthian 5:7 (NIV)

In the Bible, Ruth was an example of a woman with unwavering faith. She followed God all of her days, believing that He would provide for her. We should be taught how to be more like Ruth and have unwavering faith. In Ruth's case, having that faith in God was such a reward for her. God assured her that He would take care of her and give her all the desires if she just trusted in Him. God wants to do the same for us in return; all He asks of us is to walk in faith. As women, we are faced with many challenges so we should always have and keep the habit of walking in faith; knowing that God will see us through those challenges. 2 Corinthians 5:7 says, *"For we walk by faith, not by sight."*

My walk in faith began November 30, 2016 when my children and I were involved in a tragic car accident. Half of my body was ejected out of my SUV and crushed underneath my SUV and the other car that hit us. This tragic accident left me in a coma on life support. After almost a week in a coma, I woke up not knowing what happened to me or where my kids were. Also, sustaining a Traumatic Brain Injury (TBI) as a result from this accident had caused me to suffer severe memory loss as well as affect my ability to walk, talk, and do the things I normally did on a daily basis. My faith was never tested to this extreme, and honestly I did not know if I was going to make it out of this alive, yet I held on to my faith. I laid in my ICU bed on life support wanting to give up. I couldn't understand why God allowed such a tragedy as this to happen to me and my children who were also hospitalized.

I would cry out and ask God to please give me back the faith I had all my life. But, I felt like God wasn't listening. I would lay in ICU feeling like these were my last days on earth. However, on December 6, 2016 the doctors attempted to take me off of life support. As they turned off the machine and walked out of my room, lying there feeling lifeless and hopeless, I tried to breathe on my own but just couldn't do it. Or should I say I didn't have the **faith** to do it.

I felt as if my body was departing this world when a bright blinding light entered my room and a calm trusting voice said, *"Trust Me my child, BREATHE. Have faith in ME! It's not your time yet, BREATHE!"* At that very moment, I knew this was no one but God who was giving me life again and pouring His faith back into me! Just knowing and believing that God has all power and will pull us through any situation is creating a habit of walking in faith!

Affirmation: I will trust God and walk by faith and not by my own site.

What do I need to surrender in order to incorporate this godly habit into my Christian walk?

What are some areas in my life I need to surrender to God and walk in faith?

Reflections:

Prayer Focus: Ask God to order your steps as you walk in faith and not be moved by the things you see. Amen

THE HABIT OF STAYING IN THE CENTER OF GOD'S WILL

Melquita Singleton

"Trust in the Lord with all your heart and lean not on your own understanding; in all your ways submit to him, and he will make your paths straight."

- Proverbs 3:5-6 (NIV)

God saved my life so I owe it to Him to always give Him praise. Because of my testimony, I can say I am stronger by staying in the center of God's will. It wasn't easy for me but I knew it was necessary. Oftentimes, my flesh wanted to give up or just do things its way; however, staying in God's helped me to stand strong.

As believers, we must stay centered with God and accept His will. During my healing process after my car accident, learning how to walk, talk, think, even tie my shoe laces, I had to stay centered in God's will in order to make it through. Through much discouragement, I had to hold on tight to God's hand and trust Him. I was still praying every day that God would heal my body, take the pain away, *and* restore my faith in Him.

One day, I asked God, *"Why me?"* And He literally said, *"I heard you cry out for Me long before this accident but I had to get your attention, allowing you to feel and know that I am real and you must always trust in Me; I won't fail you."* I knew God wouldn't have allowed all these things to happen to me and not recover from it all. God told me if I stayed in the center of His will, everything would be alright.

When released from the hospital, I went to therapy almost every day, and still needed home care. I stayed with my mother who cared for me physically, mentally, emotionally, while keeping me spiritually grounded. This was exactly what I needed for my healing process due to the damages the car accident caused. God kept saying to me, *"Stay centered in My will. I will get you through this."*

Through my recovery process I realized that sometimes God has a way of showing us just what we need even if we can't see it ourselves. God wants us to stay grounded, and centered in Him, and trust that His will be done in our lives. He turned my tragedy into triumph! Today, I exude the habit of walking in faith and staying in the center of God's will due to the personal relationship I encountered with Him. I will now and forever testify to having faith in God and staying centered in His will and encourage you to do the same. God allowed me to live and share my testimony with each of you because there's no test without a testimony. I encourage you to walk in faith and stay centered in God's will!

Affirmation: I will trust in the Lord until I die.

What do I need to surrender in order to incorporate this godly habit into my Christian walk?

_____

_____

_____

_____

In what areas am I most vulnerable to Satan's attacks?

_____

_____

_____

Reflections:

_____

_____

_____

_____

Prayer Focus: Dear God, I come before You today with thanks and total praise. God, I pray that You give me the strength needed to hold on and walk in Your faith, always staying centered in Your will, Lord. In Jesus Name, Amen

THE HABIT OF FORGIVING YOURSELF

Lineshia Arrick

"Therefore, if anyone is in Christ, the new creation has come: The old has gone, the new is here! All this is from God, who reconciled us to himself through Christ and gave us the ministry of reconciliation."

- 2 Corinthians 5:17-18 (NIV)

Have you dealt with tragedy? As a believer, depression, anxiety, and tragedy are things life throws at us. The feelings that come along with tragic events can cause us to spiral into dark places which can make it hard to forgive ourselves and others. This is a trick of the adversary (the devil) that throws us off the course of our true purpose. We must remember the enemy comes to kill, steal, and to destroy.

Even when Jesus has forgiven you of your sins, sometimes it can be hard and you still can't forgive yourself. This happens many times. You tell yourself, "I know what I did, and I just can't forgive myself." Then you become paralyzed and can't move forward. You can't move forward because you can't forgive yourself.

Christ teaches us to cast all of our cares on Him. 1 Peter 5:7 says, *"Give all your worries and cares to God, for He cares about you."* Imagine if you are playing darts and you miss the target, but you keep trying because you are determined to hit it. You finally hit the target and you keep going because now you have a sense of where to aim in order to keep hitting the target. This is just how the adversary thinks; he keeps throwing darts at you until you fall or fold. But our job as Christians is to stand firm on His words knowing that no matter what comes our way God is with us even when we don't see Him.

Life may knock you down, but you have to decide whether to stay down or get back up. Losing my mom felt like it was my fault she was gone. I felt guilty that God chose me to live and not her. I was her right hand. During this time of grief, the enemy played with my mind so many times but I stood on 1 John 10:10. I chose life! And, today, I can encourage you to not let the devil steal your joy or your peace. He wants your mind. Forgive yourself today. Don't walk around with heavy burdens on your shoulder. Go to God in prayer. Do you know that God has already forgiven you? Walk in His forgiveness, and forgive yourself as well!

Mary Magdalene was a sinful woman but she did not let that stop her; she wanted to do something special for the King of kings, Jesus Christ. She washed His feet with her tears and He forgave her. His forgiveness allowed her to forgive herself and become one of His most faithful followers. Let's do the same! Ask God to forgive you, so you can learn to forgive yourself and effectively walk in your purpose.

Affirmation: I trust God to forgive me of my wrongdoings so I can easily forgive myself.

What do I need to surrender in order to incorporate this godly habit into my Christian walk?

_____

_____

_____

_____

What are some things I need to forgive myself for?

_____

_____

_____

Reflections:

_____

_____

_____

_____

Prayer Focus: I serve oppression, depression, and unforgiveness notice in the name of Jesus to flee now. I have the victory and forgive myself in Jesus name. Amen.

THE HABIT OF BEARING GOOD FRUIT

Lineshia Arrick

"But the fruit of the Spirit is love, joy, peace, forbearance, kindness, goodness, faithfulness, gentleness and self-control..."

- Galatians 5:22-23 (NIV)

In life, good and bad happens, but what we have control over is how we respond to them. Our love language is the center of it all. Reading God's word, and having an intimate relationship with Him, will enable you to bear good fruit. If our lives get cluttered with things that get in the way of our relationship with God, we won't produce the fruit God wants from us.

In your life you won't be able to pick the trails you go through; it's a process. The way you handle these things, however, shows spiritual growth. The flesh is weak; it will always want you to go back to your old way of thinking.

Following Christ is not an easy road, but definitely worth it.

Being a Christian is NOT something you can do on your own. You can do good deeds of your own free will, you can be a nice person if you want to be, but you can't be Christ-like without some help from Him. God's nature is love, so everything He does in our lives will come from that very place. God wants us to surrender to Him, giving Him our whole heart. We must have child-like spirits when it comes to Christ.

What fruit should we be bearing? The fruit of the Spirit – love, joy, peace, patience, kindness, goodness, faithfulness, gentleness, and self-control. But, first and foremost is love! John says in his first letter that we should "love one another, because love is from God; everyone who loves is born of God and knows God."

Positioning yourself for what God has for you should always be your portion. Patience is giving others grace: loving even when mistakes are made. Patience for His timing is not ours. Jesus is our first example of self-control; the Bible teaches us Jesus was tempted by the devil to respond with His emotions and not to trust God's promise. Self-control is thinking before you act or speak. Thinking before we speak reassures us that what we say will come out in a loving manner. Having a spirit of humility is a portion of this fruit we must bear. God does not want us to be easily moved with anger. To be gentle, we have to humble ourselves.

Mary of Bethany is a great example of a woman who displayed the fruit of the Spirit. Her desire was to sit at Jesus' feet even when there was work to be done. The fruit is a source from God that draws us closer to Him. The role of the fruit is to spread seeds and allow the plant to reproduce. Reading God's Word and having a relationship with Him will keep your plant watered.

Affirmation: I will trust God in all I do; He is my source.

What do I need to surrender in order to incorporate this godly habit into my Christian walk?

_____

_____

_____

_____

What are some ways I can demonstrate bearing good fruit?

_____

_____

_____

Reflections:

_____

_____

_____

_____

Prayer Focus: Father God, thank You for showing me what true love looks like. Please perfect me in Your love by showing me the parts of my life that are not in line with Your Holy Spirit. In Jesus name, Amen.

THE HABIT OF FASTING AND PRAYING

Dawn Pullin

*"And Jesus said unto them, Because of your
unbelief: for verily I say unto you, If ye have faith
as a grain of mustard seed, ye shall say unto this
mountain..."*

- Matthew 17:20-21 (KJV)

God desires to have consistent communication with His
people daily. We should view fasting and praying just as
important as serving God as it brings forth a great
manifestation of the Lord's will for our lives. Prayer and
fasting develops intimacy between you and God that
provides opportunity for God to move mightily in and
through your life. You should set aside specific time for
prayer and fasting. Prayer and fasting should be
intentional and done with expectation.

Fasting is denying oneself from people, places, and things that distract us from focusing on God. In the Bible, many times people fasted from food in order to deny their flesh and to show God they were willing to sacrifice something they depended on daily and only He could sustain them.

The Bible tells us to pray without ceasing because prayer keeps the lines of communication open at all times. Prayer is the place where we can speak to God but also where God speaks to us. Communication is vital when it comes to building a relationship with God and others. We have to be open to give and receive information and fasting helps us to open our mind, heart, and spirit to receive from heaven through prayer. We should set time aside for prayer daily and we should not just pray to ask for things, but seek God for direction, guidance, and answers to our everyday life concerns.

Two women in the Bible that understood and depended on fasting and prayer were Hannah and Anna. They both sought God in prayer in the hard times and they not only believed but trusted God and waited for the manifestation of what they prayed for. Prayer and fasting are essential in daily life. If we want to live a life based on the promises of God, we must fast and pray to stay connected to Him and to receive His divine instructions.

Affirmation: I am a prayer warrior who believes in fasting.

What do I need to surrender in order to incorporate this godly habit into my Christian walk?

_____

_____

_____

_____

What are your thoughts on fasting? Do you believe that fasting is necessary?

_____

_____

_____

Reflections:

_____

_____

_____

_____

Prayer Focus: Lord, teach me how to fast and pray so that I can hear from heaven and receive from you what I need to sustain myself daily. Amen

THE HABIT OF SELF-CONTROL

Dawn Pullin

"For the grace of God has appeared that offers salvation to all people. It teaches us to say "No" to ungodliness and worldly passions, and to live self-controlled, upright and godly lives in this present age."

- Titus 2:11-12 (NIV)

Self-control is defined as one's ability to control oneself, in particular one's emotions and desires or the expression of them in one's behavior, especially in difficult situations. Self-control can be described as self-discipline, self-restraint, control, self-mastery, self-possession, and will power. The habit of self-control is so important for believers but especially for women of God.

Self-control is a portion of the fruit of the spirit which means it's a characteristic and an attribute of God. We are talking about the ability to control oneself when it pertains to our emotions, desires, and how we express them in positive and negative manners to bring forth desired outcomes.

We as women of God have to understand we can't do this on our own or in our will power. We have to connect our will to the will of God to obtain and maintain self-control. Through us, God desires to show unbelievers who He is so they will desire to know Him on a greater level. Being a woman who exhibits self-control or discipline in your personal, professional, and spiritual life gives others the opportunity to see God working through you.

In James 1:19, it states that we must all be quick to listen, slow to speak, and slow to get angry. Understanding that when we profess to walk with God we must exemplify who He is at all times. This does not mean we can't express our thoughts, emotions, and feelings; it means we will not allow them to control our response to people, places, and situations.

We must learn to seek God in the hard places, the places where our emotions and feelings want to rule. We must allow God's will to abide in us in such a way that the spirit of God has permission to rise in every situation. Our flesh must stay under subjection of the spirit to the point that we allow *His* will to be done. We must practice self-control in every circumstance and be guided by the spirit so the Glory of God is revealed in all situations.

Abigail is the epitome of a godly woman who, under difficult circumstances and a challenging marriage, demonstrated her strength through her ability to maintain self-control. Abigail's ability to control her actions, emotions, and words with grace showed self-control. Her faith in God always enabled her to control her words and choose them wisely. We too must be like Abigail and adopt this godly habit in order to effectively walk in our purpose!

Affirmation: God, I release my self-control and exchange it for Your will so that the Holy Spirit will guide my words, thoughts and deeds from this day forward.

What do I need to surrender in order to incorporate this godly habit into my Christian walk?

_____

_____

_____

What do I need to do daily to ensure that I have surrendered my self-control to the Holy Spirit?

_____

_____

_____

Reflections:

_____

_____

_____

_____

Prayer Focus: Ask God to show you how to exchange your will for His will in every situation.

THE HABIT OF STANDING AGAINST THE ENEMY

Gilana Pearce

"But I say to you who hear, Love your enemies, do good to those who hate you, bless those who curse you, pray for those who abuse you."

- Luke 6:27-28 (NIV)

Jael was a powerful woman of God, a homemaker to be exact. We tend to rate someone's anointing and assignment in Christ by how loud and boisterous they are. I don't care where you started or if your upbringing wasn't grand and you didn't have the best of things in your eyes; it will never discount what God called you to do.

People get it twisted, but don't ever mistake position with power! Pride is what makes you think you need to respond with "clapback" words. Our job is to continue to follow God's principles and love regardless.

The enemy is strategic, and you can be as well with God's direction. We have to renew our minds daily, and with so much entitlement, unrest and anger, everyone is a possible enemy, whether over political views, judgmental posts on social media, or comments that try to distract you from your purpose and destiny. You have to know who you are when people try to speak anything over your life other than what God spoke over you in your mother's womb.

There are people waiting on you to stand against the enemy and lead by example, with courage and wisdom. You will be blessed for handling the enemy the right way. I know you've probably heard the saying "kill them with kindness." That's kind of what Jael did. Now, don't do what Jael did in the natural when someone does you wrong. God will give you a way to stand that will confuse the enemy. Anytime you are doing something great and especially for God, the enemy is coming.

Marvin Sapp said it best (my paraphrase), *"If the enemy is giving you a hard time, just know he saw a glimpse of your future."* He will do anything to distract you from reaching your goal. Stay focused on your assignment. If you don't fuss back or seek retaliation with people in a negative manner, they can't argue with themselves. Don't block your blessings with foolishness!

Affirmation: I will study God's word to get instructions on how to effectively stand against the enemy.

What do I need to surrender in order to incorporate this godly habit into my Christian walk?

_____

_____

_____

In what area am I most vulnerable to Satan's attacks? What are some ways this godly habit speaks to me?

_____

_____

_____

Reflections:

_____

_____

_____

Prayer Focus: Lord, I thank You that you have already given me the strength to stand against the enemy humbly regardless of title, stature and position in society. Amen.

THE HABIT OF RESISTING TEMPTATION

Gilana Pearce

"Watch and pray so that you will not fall into temptation. The spirit is willing, but the flesh is weak."

- Matthew 26:41 (NIV)

There is so much significance resisting temptation. Eve had an issue with this, and as you know, it affected lots of people. Just one action broke covenant, destroyed trust in relationships, *and* caused a generational curse that still lives to today. You know that little thing about pain in childbirth? Yep, that was one consequence of not resisting temptation.

Ok, so in all seriousness, we are no different. Our choices change the outcomes of things with children, spouses, relationships and health. When we choose to do what we want instead of His purpose, we cause generational curses and lack. If we are unfaithful to our husbands, we leave sorrow in a family, we leave a lack of wholeness with our kids, we cause distrust in our love life, and because they don't want to end up like Mommy and Daddy, they may want to experience promiscuity to find love in all the wrong places.

The stress of abuse, separation or divorce causes health issues. Stress can bring on heart attacks, strokes, depression and anxiety to name a few. It causes the other person to doubt themselves and brings a lack of self-confidence even if they think they were good enough. On the contrary, resisting temptation can bring peace of mind, fulfillment in relationships and marriages without emotional baggage. If thousands of years ago Eve's choice is felt today, imagine what ripple you can leave in this world resisting temptation.

Affirmation: I am done with mind games that will keep me from my purpose and God's destiny for my life.

What do I need to surrender in order to incorporate this godly habit into my Christian walk?

_____

_____

Why am I really afraid to trust God and give Him my YES and walk in my purpose?

_____

_____

_____

Reflections:

_____

_____

Prayer Focus: Thank You God for giving me revelation and understanding of Your Word so I know who I am in You. I WILL NOT be moved by anything that does not serve my purpose and Your destiny for my life. I thank You for a renewed mind and the desire to hide Your Word in my heart that I may resist the enemy. In Jesus name, Amen.

THE HABIT OF RELEASING

Gilana Pearce

"Immediately Jesus, recognizing in Himself that power had gone out from Him, turned around in the crowd and asked, "Who touched My clothes?"

- Mark 5:30 (MSG)

Cast your burden on the Lord [release it] and He will sustain and uphold *you*; He will never allow the righteous to be shaken (slip, fall, fail) Psalms 55:22 AMP

Releasing is a powerful action. The habit to release frees you to walk in victory and let go of things keeping you stuck in life (career, relationship, parenting, etc.) What if the hurt you experienced in life never healed causing you to mistreat family and you passed that trauma to them through unforgiveness, hatred, and promiscuity? These are generational curses that need to be broken through releasing!

Career: you cannot seem to get promoted because you hold anger and have a quick temper because you've had something bottled up for years.

Relationship: you can't love or be loved because you never forgave and never released a prior person in past relationships (molestation, unfaithfulness, etc.) so you have unnecessary baggage that does not benefit you at all.

Parenting: you are yelling and screaming because that is what you heard and now you can't communicate effectively because you want to have some sense of control and your child is looking for love in the wrong places because of it.

When we release what we have and who we are to Jesus, wonderful things happen. It is amazing what Jesus does when we release control to Him...past hurts and failures, fears, self-centered needs, and so much more. When you are finally able to grasp this truth, you will no longer find yourself complaining when something bad is going on in your life. Instead of being negative and critical, you will find yourself turning to •God in prayer and lifting your hands in worship to the One who loves you more than anyone else on the face of this earth. You will find yourself being caught up in the presence of a holy God and you will experience a new release of His anointing and glory in your life.

Just like the woman with the issue of blood, she carried this condition for a long time! It did not benefit her and it was not until she got sick and tired her freedom came.

Releasing things takes humbling yourself to get low enough to bring about change. She pressed through the crowd past all negative comments (family, friends, thoughts and pre-conceived notions) of what would happen by touching the hem of Jesus' garment. Her faith was so powerful, virtue left Jesus' body when she touched Him. When was the last time you released your faith enough to touch Jesus and get His attention.

Affirmation: I will release those things that don't benefit me
and walk in freedom of release.

What do I need to surrender in order to incorporate this
godly habit into my Christian walk?

_____

_____

_____

What's one excuse I'm ready to stop giving in order to
adopt this godly habit and walk in my purpose??

_____

_____

_____

Reflections:

_____

_____

_____

_____

*Prayer Focus: Lord, help me to release so I can walk in
freedom and obtain what You have for me in all areas of
my life. I understand this is a daily journey, but it is
possible with You. In Jesus name, Amen!*

THE HABIT OF CARING

Cynthia Rucker-Collins

"For I was hungry and you gave me something to eat, I was thirsty and you gave me something to drink, I was a stranger and you invited me in…"

- Matthew 25:35-36 (NIV)

The godly habit of caring is important in the body of Christ because caring should be shown by your love for others. In the Merriam–Webster dictionary, caring means: "feeling or showing concern for or kindness to others." How you treat others reflects your love for Christ.

The scripture tells us to feed the hungry, clothe the naked, visit the sick- this godly habit of caring displays loves to others. Christians' love is different from the world's love- because what we do is for God to get the glory. It is not about us, but rather to be a blessing to someone else.

God gave His only begotten Son because He loved and cared about our salvation. Jesus died on the cross because He loved us so much and He did not want us to die in our sins.

The godly habit of caring lets the world know that we are the hands and feet of Jesus and we care about people. Whatever we do in word or deed brings glory to God.

Show someone you care about them today because it may just be what they need to get through a tough situation. Your encouraging words may bring peace to someone that may want to give up.

Affirmation: With God's help I am capable, compassionate, and caring.

What do I need to surrender in order to incorporate this godly habit into my Christian walk?

_____

_____

_____

If I already possess this godly habit, how can I use it to be more effective in my walk with God?

_____

_____

_____

Reflections:

_____

_____

_____

_____

Prayer Focus: Ask God to remind you that your role is to care for others around you, and focus on those who need your help and not be judgmental, as we are all equal in God's eyes.

THE HABIT OF CONTENTMENT

Cynthia Rucker-Collins

"Keep your lives free from the love of money and be content with what you have, because God has said, "Never will I leave you; never will I forsake you.""

- Hebrews 13:5 (NIV)

I have been at a point of despair, and I did not know what to do. God always provided for me and my family. It was hard as a single mother to raise 3 children alone, but God provided. The godly habit of contentment delivered me from worrying. Whenever you go through trials and tribulations God will be there with you. Sometimes we do not see the answer right then, but God is working it out behind the scenes.

My favorite scripture is Proverbs 3:5-6 (NIV) *"Trust in the Lord with all your heart and lean not on your own understanding; in all your ways submit to him, and he will make your paths straight."* I had to learn to lean and trust in God when my finances were low along with many other things. As a Christian, we can become so focused on the wrong things in life; however, when we apply the godly habit of contentment it will make a difference in our life.

Jesus was at a woman named Martha's house and she was worried about preparations that had to be made. Luke 10:40 (NIV): *"But Martha was distracted by all the preparations that had to be made. She came to him and asked, "Lord, don't you care that my sister has left me to do the work by myself?"* Luke 10:41-42 (NIV) *"Martha, Martha,"* the Lord answered, *"You are worried and upset about many things, but few things are needed – or indeed only one. Mary has chosen what is better, and it will not be taken away from her."*

When we please God He will provide for us, because we are not to take any thought for tomorrow. It is hard sometimes to trust God, especially when your back is against the wall. God said He will never leave us nor forsake us. He has a plan for your life, so do not give up!

Affirmation: I am content with the life God has given me and will honor Him in all I do.

What do I need to surrender in order to incorporate this godly habit into my Christian walk?

_____

_____

_____

What can I do to spend more time in God's presence to gain direction to walk in my purpose?

_____

_____

_____

Reflections:

_____

_____

_____

Prayer Focus: Ask God to help you adopt an attitude of gratefulness for all He has given you.

THE HABIT OF OBEYING GOD

Cynthia Rucker-Collins

"But I gave them this command: Obey me, and I will be your God and you will be my people. Walk in obedience to all I command you that it may go well with you."

- Jeremiah 7:23 (NIV)

How much do you love God? When you love someone, it is shown by your actions not just by words. Love is a powerful action that brings great rewards, and the godly habit of obeying God brings abundant blessings. When a person has the godly habit of obedience to God it brings peace, joy, and purpose.

This godly habit of obeying God will bring favor and protection over your life. In the book Esther, Esther obtained favor from the king to see him on behalf of the Jews. She had not been granted permission to see the king, but she was willing to save her nation, Esther 4:14

says, *"For if you remain completely silent at this time, relief and deliverance will arise for the Jews from another place, but you and your father's house will perish. Yet who knows whether you have come into the kingdom for such a time as this?"*

She was able to save a nation from destruction from an evil man. She knew God had prepared her for such a time as this. Once we recognize the call of God, we must then decide whether or not to believe God can enable us to do what He is calling us to be a part of. Having affirmed our faith in the Lord, we then adjust our lives in order to be in a position to obey. Obedience is crucial, for without it, we will never do the will of God and experience His working in our lives.

When you have the godly habit of obeying God, He will direct your path. In crisis situations, you will need wisdom. Every moment we hesitate to follow the call of God, is a moment we risk wandering around in darkness. Every moment we hesitate to follow the call of God is a moment we risk wasting our life, rather than investing our life! Therefore, we need to commit ourselves to living our life, walking in whatever light God has given us to walk in to effectively carry out our purpose.

Esther knew she could not approach the king without God's favor upon her life. She fasted and prayed for 3 days before she stepped out to approach the king. Our answers to prayers come when we seek God with all our heart and mind.

Affirmation: I won't just listen to God's Word; I will do what it says.

What do I need to surrender in order to incorporate this godly habit into my Christian walk?

_____

_____

_____

Every Christian should obey God. What's the first step you need to take to adopt this godly habit to effectively walk in your purpose?

_____

_____

_____

Reflections:

_____

_____

_____

Prayer Focus: Ask God to help you trust and depend on Him in every area of your life. Listen to the voice of God and He will direct your path.

THE HABIT OF TAKING CONTROL OF YOUR MIND

Evette Corbin

"Summing it all up, friends, I'd say you'll do best by filling your minds and meditating on things true, noble, reputable, authentic, compelling, gracious—the best, not the worst; the beautiful, not the ugly; things to praise, not things to curse."

- Philippians 4:8 (MSG)

"What if? When will this end? How much longer? Does anyone really care?" are questions we often ask ourselves when life deals us disappointments and hope seems a long way off. How do we corral those wayward thoughts that seem to gallop freely with no restraints through our minds and kick up a dust storm of lies and untruths that God does not love us?

The woman with the issue of blood had every reason to be consumed with negative thoughts. She suffered for twelve long years, spending time and money on doctors and cures, only to be disappointed each time. While we may not be bleeding internally, our negative thoughts can drain us of hope and strength. Each time we dwell on the past or tell ourselves *"we're not good enough, smart enough, attractive enough, or spiritual enough,"* we bleed a little more.

One day though, she found herself in a crowd with Jesus and said to herself, *"If I only touch the hem of his garment, I will be healed."* Did you catch that? *"She said to herself!"* Sometimes we have to speak to ourselves and change the narrative in our minds. What we tell ourselves impact our emotions, behaviors, and actions. In that pivotal moment, thoughts of life, healing, and faith flooded her mind, and crowded out the fear and doubt that nothing would ever change. With renewed hope and determination, she reached out and touched Jesus. Immediately she was completely and totally healed.

Philippians 4:8 encourages us to think on whatsoever things are true, honest, just, pure, lovely, and of good report. "Think" in this context means to consider and take into account, and implies that we have a choice on what we focus on. Why is this important? Because these kinds of thoughts are God-honoring and life-producing and negate the lies the enemy would have us believe. When we renew our minds with God's truth, we can confidently face every challenge and trial, knowing that God is not only with us but for us.

Now, that's a thought habit to actively meditate on and to practice daily.

Affirmation: God, I release my self-control and exchange it for Your will so that the Holy Spirit will guide my words, thoughts and deeds from this day forward.

What do I need to surrender in order to incorporate this godly habit into my Christian walk?

_____

_____

_____

What's one lie I'm ready to stop believing about myself so that I can walk in my purpose?

_____

_____

_____

Reflections:

_____

_____

_____

_____

Prayer Focus: Lord, I submit my thoughts to You. Help me to stay focused on that which pleases Your heart. In Jesus' name Amen.

THE HABIT OF GRACE

Evette Corbin

"Let us then approach God's throne of grace with confidence, so that we may receive mercy and find grace to help us in our time of need."

- Hebrews 4:16 (NIV)

Have you ever wished that you could start the day or year over again after making some questionable choices and decisions? If so, you are not alone.

Imagine the woman caught committing adultery. Her life choices, her sin and shame were evident for all to see. With judgment in their hearts, the crowd and religious leaders were ready to stone her, and rightfully so according to the Levitical law. Yet on that day, grace showed up.

Grace is God's unmerited favor; it's when we don't get what we deserve. Someone once said that GRACE is an acronym for God's Riches At Christ's Expense. Grace includes God's forgiveness, mercy, and goodness, all wrapped up in His love, and provides a means to begin again.

Jesus asked the woman, *"Where are your accusers? Has no one condemned you?"* She slowly and hesitantly looked around, saw only the dropped stones, and whispered, *"No one."* Jesus compassionately and tenderly replied, *"Neither do I. Go and sin no more."* The only One that could condemn her offered her forgiveness and a new start to life.

That's grace. None of us are perfect and all of us have weaknesses. When we know that we have failed, made a mess of things, and would rather run from God, He offers us grace and the choice to start over with a renewed heart and purpose.

Let's make it a daily habit to extend grace to ourselves and to others.

Affirmation: God, I release my self-control and exchange it for Your will so that the Holy Spirit will guide my words, thoughts and deeds from this day forward.

What do I need to surrender in order to incorporate this godly habit into my Christian walk?

_____

_____

_____

_____

What is one revelation God shared with me after reading this content?

_____

_____

_____

Reflections:

_____

_____

_____

_____

Prayer Focus: Lord, I thank You for the grace that You give to me each and every day. Amen.

THE HABIT OF JOY

Evette Corbin

"You make known to me the path of life; you will fill me with joy in your presence, with eternal pleasures at your right hand."

- Psalms 16:11 (NIV)

Let me ask you a question. How often do you think of joy? On a scale of 1 – 10, what's your joy-o-meter registering? With everything that is happening in this world and all the responsibilities you have, it may be challenging at times to think of joy, let alone experience it. Yet joy is so needed.

Joy means cheerfulness, delight, and gladness. It is different from happiness which is often dependent on external circumstances. It is a gift from the Lord and comes from abiding in His presence.

In Luke 10: 38 – 42, Jesus came to the home of Mary and Martha, the sisters of Lazarus. The consummate hostess that she was, Martha wanted everything to be perfect. I can imagine how she rushed from room to room, prepping the food, arranging the furniture, and fluffing the pillows for the honored guest. What should have been a joyous occasion caused Martha to be distracted and overwhelmed. Although Jesus was present in the house, Martha, in her frenzy, did not experience joy being in the presence of Jesus.

Though Mary was aware of what needed to be done in her home, she chose rather to sit at the feet of Jesus, being still and attentive to her Lord. For this she was commended. This one intentional decision brought much joy and contentment to Mary's heart, which could not be taken away from her.

On a daily basis, there will be many responsibilities, obligations, and distractions that call for our attention. In these times, joy seems fleeting, like a guest that's more of a stranger than a constant companion. In the midst of our hectic lives, know that Jesus is right there in our homes, seeing all the tasks to be done. Still, He lovingly beckons us to sit at His feet and experience the full joy of being in His presence. That's a habit I want to keep.

Affirmation: I will enjoy every moment of my life and be thankful for all I have.

What do I need to surrender in order to incorporate this godly habit into my Christian walk?

_____

_____

_____

What are some ways this godly habit speaks to me? What are some things I can do to decide to be filled with JOY?

_____

_____

_____

Reflections:

_____

_____

_____

_____

Prayer Focus: Lord, help me to know this joy of being in Your presence. Amen.

THE HABIT OF RESILIENCE

Dr. Anastasia Freeborn

"'For I know the plans I have for you,' declares the Lord, 'plans to prosper you and not to harm you, plans to give you hope and a future."

- Jeremiah 29:11 (NIV)

Has there been a time in your life when circumstances seemed to be working against you, and the status quo just wasn't in your favor? A time when you knew you were entitled to something, but powers that be put up a big STOP sign?

The greatest women of the Bible were not super people but they had great resilience. To be resilient means you are a person with an ability to bounce back from defeats, discouragements, or hardships. It does not mean you won't go through things in life, nor experience day-to-day challenges. It means you will have the tenacity, strength, and courage to work through the physical, emotional, and mental pain and suffering you may endure. Spiritual resiliency is a godly habit all women must possess to effectively walk in your purpose!

In the book of Numbers, we learn of five sisters who didn't stop until they got what they knew was theirs. They were bold, faithful, and resilient. The daughters of Zelophehad were named Mahlah, Noah, Hoglah, Milcah and Tirzah. They were all single women, unmarried. When Zelophehad died in the wilderness, leaving no sons, it left his only daughters as descendants, and they felt greatly disenfranchised. Under Jewish law women didn't have the right to inherit property. The sisters could have simply lived with their lamentation, but they were resilient. They came up with a bold strategy. They audaciously approached Moses, Eleazar the high priest, and the entire leadership of the nation of Israel. The daughters told the tribunal, *"Let not our father's name be lost to his clan just because he had no son! Give us a holding among our father's kinsmen!"* (Numbers 27:4). Moses listened to their case, and he went to God on their behalf, and God told Moses the women were right! The law was amended and they received their inheritance.

In a world of complacency and self-satisfaction, a world where many have become o.k. with the familiar, we often find it easier to give up than strive to become the best we can be. God is calling you to be a woman with a habit of resilience who isn't afraid to reach for greatness. We are a chosen generation. What we choose to do with our lives today will not affect our ancestors, but it will certainly affect our descendants.

God knew these five daughters would make their case to Moses before they even set out for the tent of meeting. They were relentless, bold, tenacious, confident, courageous, and resilient. Life isn't always fair, but God has your back. As you go on with resilience, as did Zelophehad's daughters, God will honor your commitment with beautiful blessings.

Affirmation: I am a survivor because I can do all things through Christ Who strengthens me.

What do I need to surrender in order to incorporate this godly habit into my Christian walk?

_____

_____

_____

What areas in your life do you need assurance from God?

_____

_____

_____

Reflections:

_____

_____

_____

Prayer Focus: Ask God to show You His many blessings, your inheritance, and pray for boldness in stepping out in faith.

THE HABIT OF LAYING ASIDE EVERY WEIGHT

Dr. Anastasia Freeborn

"Therefore, since we are surrounded by such a great cloud of witnesses, let us throw off everything that hinders and the sin that so easily entangles. And let us run with perseverance the race marked out for us."

- Hebrews 12:1 (NIV)

To lay aside means to put away, to cast off, to lay down. The word "every" means all, any, every, the whole enchilada, not part of it. The word "weight" signifies a burden or a hindrance.

As Christians, we must learn to put away and cast off all burdens, hindrances, and offences that can so easily cause us to be stagnant. If we are stagnant, then we are not running, and this is a race. You can't win a race by standing still; you must be in motion. Possessing this godly habit allows you to keep running in order to finish the race and win! We must put aside everything that has the potential to stop us from running and have us standing still in this race.

As we go through life, we must adopt godly habits that will allow us to effectively walk in our purpose. Laying aside every weight and sin allows us to press in relentlessly, and when we stumble, be able to bounce back, and try again! I used to wonder if there was an algorithm – a formula – a *habit* of getting rid of the WEIGHTY THINGS in my life. I was bound in a spiritual quagmire. Misconceptions can be a snare; my freedom was found in scripture; through an epiphany about how my language and culture supports my personal connection to God.

As an African, I wrestled with the relevancy of the Bible early in my Christian walk. I viewed it as a "western" faith. This was a weight (my misconceptions) I felt I could not put away. A weight I needed to lay aside in order to seek God and grow. Misconceptions can weigh down your heart, distract your attention, and drain your energy. They will take you out of the race. However, searching for answers to bring about a revelation, and lead me to something greater, my eyes were opened while reading Zephaniah 3:10 *"Beyond the rivers of Ethiopia my suppliants, even the daughter of my dispersed, shall bring mine offering (KJV)."* He revealed to me that I was an esteemed woman who could approach Him regardless of my ethnicity, that I had a preeminent offering.

Mary Magdalene made a conscience decision to boldly surrender her life to Christ. The Bible tells us she broke the alabaster jar and wiped Jesus' feet with her hair and tears. Her decision to repent of her sins and turn from her wrongdoings, and follow Jesus displayed her willingness to lay aside every weight and follow Him.

Do you have a *habit* or algorithm for a closer walk with God? Do you have a method to the madness of laying aside the weights in your life?

Affirmation: I will set aside every weight to successfully run the race that is set before me as a child of God.

What do I need to surrender in order to incorporate this godly habit into my Christian walk?

_____

_____

_____

Like Mary Magdalene, what habit can you practice in honoring God through your service?

_____

_____

_____

Reflections:

_____

_____

_____

Prayer Focus: Ask God to help you lay aside every weight in your life that is hindering you from walking in your purpose.

THE HABIT OF SEEKING GOD

Twylia G. Reid

"My heart says of you, "Seek his face!" Your face, Lord, I will seek."

- Psalm 27:8 (NIV)

What does it mean to seek God? Does it imply that you have lost Him? Of course not! The word "seek" appears many times in the Bible, and often it appears as a command to God's people. Sometimes the command tells us to *"seek peace and pursue it"*; sometimes the command is to *"seek righteousness or holiness."* But most times, the command simply tells us to *"seek God."* Now, why would God give those who are saved and know Him this command? Maybe, it's because although we are indeed God's children, His presence and genuineness is not always evident to us. God wants us to focus on Him in our everyday life. You see, to seek God means to familiarize ourselves with Him and to chase HIM rather than the things of this world.

The Bible tells us, *"Blessed are those who hunger and thirst for a right relationship with God, for they shall be filled."* When we wake up each day, are we hungry and thirsty? Seeking God is not something you do when you are not saved and don't know Him and then stop and never do it again because you accept Jesus as your Lord and Savior. Jesus is a person you develop a relationship with, and your knowledge of Him is never complete. Therefore, the seeking must never stop.

There are several benefits to possessing the habit of seeking God and putting Him first in your life. These benefits will far exceed what you can possibly imagine! One benefit of seeking God is peace. I don't know about you, but nothing in my life compares to the perfect peace that God **alone** can provide. When we do not seek God first pertaining to the matters of our heart, we attempt life within our own scope of knowledge. Our ways are limiting; therefore, sooner rather than later we end up in a disturbed and uneasy mindset accompanied by a lack of peace.

Another key benefit of seeking God is wisdom! Don't you know God is eager *and* willing to impart His wisdom upon us? All we have to do is ask Him. The Bible says if anyone lacks wisdom to simply ask God for it. Not only will He give it to you, but also He will give it generously without reproach! All of the powerful women in the Bible sought after God daily. They understood their assignment, the habit of seeking God, and executed it successfully. So you see it's really not that hard. Possessing the habit of seeking God is a wonderful thing. God loves you, and will give you peace, guidance, and wisdom when you seek Him. How much better to seek Him first as you encounter situations and give Him priority in allowing Him to lead the way? When you adapt to seeking God, He will bless your obedience and submission to Him beyond your wildest dream!

Affirmation: I will seek the LORD while He may be found; call on Him while He is near.

What do I need to surrender in order to incorporate this godly habit into my Christian walk?

_____

_____

_____

What are some ways I can seek God?

_____

_____

_____

Reflections:

_____

_____

_____

_____

*Prayer Focus: Ask God to help you seek His face **and** His presence continually so that your heart will rejoice always.*

THE HABIT OF LOVE

Twylia G. Reid

"Love is patient, love is kind. It does not envy, it does not boast, it is not proud. It does not dishonor others, it is not self-seeking, it is not easily angered, it keeps no record of wrongs..."

- *1 Corinthians 13:4-8 (NIV)*

When we think of love, it's easy to think about good feelings. But real love is not dependent on feelings. It is about so much more than how you feel about someone. When you can do these things for someone in spite of your feelings, regardless of their actions; that is love. When you are tempted in anger, tempted to impatience, tempted to seek your own way of doing things, tempted to believe the worst in others, and to give up on someone, this is not true love. But when you deny these feelings and rejoice, become long-suffering, begin to humble yourself, become patient with others no matter what, then you are operating in true love.

The pure love of Christ, which is charity, inspires us not only to act and provide service, but also to have the strength to forgive, regardless of the situation. Christianity in its essence is all about relationship between God and man. This relationship is cultivated through love exchanged between God and man. God is love. Man is not. Man therefore is urged in the first great command to "love the Lord your God with all your heart." However, the command does not end with love exchange between God and man. A second great command is issued by Jesus Christ in the gospels: "Love your neighbor as yourself." What does it mean to love your neighbor as yourself?

When it comes to real love, God's love never fails. God never stops loving us. His love is unconditional and He never gives up on us. It doesn't matter what we do, who we are, or what our status is. God loves us all the same. One of the best things about God's love is that it is universal. He has compassion on both believers and unbelievers. Additionally, one of the most important features that makes God love so special is that it motivates us to do good. As Christian women, we must strive to love others as Christ loves us. This will allow us to see past the faults of others and love *them* unconditionally.

Taking on this godly habit will assist you in understanding what love truly is as you learn to love the way the Bible teaches us to love. There are no exceptions to love. Agape love that is! All of the great women in the Bible possessed the habit of love. Esther, Mary the mother of Jesus, Hannah, Sarah, Mary Magdalene, Elizabeth, Rachel, Ruth, and so many more! Jesus laid down His life for us, the ultimate sign of how much He loved us. As women of God, it our duty to show others the same degree of love as we effectively walk in our God-given purpose impacting lives one person at a time.

Affirmation: I have an infinite supply of love to give and receive.

What do I need to surrender in order to incorporate this godly habit into my Christian walk?

_____

_____

_____

_____

What are some ways I can demonstrate more love to others?

_____

_____

_____

Reflections:

_____

_____

_____

_____

Prayer Focus: Ask God to help you love others the way He demonstrates His love for you. Amen.

THE HABIT OF RESPONSIBILITY

Twylia G. Reid

"When I was a child, I talked like a child, I thought like a child, I reasoned like a child. When I became a man, I put the ways of childhood behind me."

- 1 Corinthians 13:11(NIV)

Being responsible means more than taking initiative. Our behavior is a function of our decisions, not our conditions. "Response-ability" is the _ability_ to choose your _response_! Get it? A responsible woman doesn't blame her circumstances, her conditions, or her conditioning for her behavior. Your behavior is a product of your own conscious choice.... based on your values.

We all have the freedom to choose! Therefore, responsible people focus their energies on their circle of influence. They work on the things they can do something about rather on things they know they can't control. Possessing the habit of responsibility allows you to demonstrate responsible behavior, you know, doing what you should do in any situation; even when it's not easy, fun, or clear. Making the right choices, identifying and accepting the consequences of your decisions...the good, the bad, and the ugly! In the long run, it means considering how your actions will affect people and situations around you.

No one's perfect. Being responsible doesn't mean that you never make a mistake. But it does mean that you are willing to acknowledge when you blow it. It means that you accept the consequences and try to do better. No one does the right thing all the time. Sometimes it's really hard to do the responsible thing. It's okay to make mistakes. Striving to be a person other people can count on is a worthy goal. Being true to yourself makes you someone you and others can respect and admire.

The Bible shows us two Hebrew midwives, Shiphrah and Puah, who definitely possessed the habit of responsibility. They show us what doing right in God's eyes truly looks like. The king of Egypt had ordered these two Hebrew midwives to kill all the Hebrew boys when they were born. These women feared God more than this king who could have easily had them killed. Instead, they lied and said the babies were born before they arrived. Their habit of responsibility demonstrated their ability to choose their response, which in turned saved many children's lives! They knew what they did in God's eyes mattered most in spite of facing the hard choice they were given. No one does the right thing all the time. Sometimes it's really hard to do the responsible thing. It's okay to make mistakes. Striving to be a person other people can count on is a worthy goal. Being true to yourself makes you someone you and others can respect and admire.

Affirmation: I am responsible for everything in my life.

What do I need to surrender in order to incorporate this godly habit into my Christian walk? How will this make me better?

What are some things I can do to up my responsibility game and effectively walk in my purpose?

Reflections:

Prayer Focus: Ask God to help you accept responsibility for all of your life choices. Amen.

"She opens her mouth with wisdom, and the teaching of kindness is on her tongue."

- Proverbs 31:26

NAMES OF GOD

God has shown Himself to us in the Holy Scriptures by many different names. As we understand the names of God, we can and will gain a better understanding of His nature and character so that we might come to know Him more, and grow our relationship with the Name above all names!

"Because he has set his love upon Me, therefore I will deliver him; I will set him on high, because he has known My name." Psalm 91:14

Elohim - God of Creation (Genesis 1)

Jehovah – God of redemption and revelation (Exodus 3:14)

Adonai – Master (Exodus 4:10, 13)

El Elyon – "the most high God" (Genesis 14:18)

El Olam – "the Everlasting God" (Genesis 21:33)

El Shaddai – "the Almighty God" (Genesis 17:1)

Jehovah Jireh – "the LORD will provide" (Genesis 22:14)

Jehovah Nissi – "the LORD our banner" (Exodus 17:8-15)

Jehovah Shalom – "the LORD our peace" (Judges 6:23-24)

Jehovah Sabbaoth – "the LORD of hosts" (I Samuel 1:3)

Jehovah Maccaddeshcem – "the LORD your sanctifier" (Exodus 31:13)

Jehovah Roi – "the LORD is my shepherd" (Psalm 23:1)

Jehovah Tsidkenu – "the LORD our righteousness" (Jeremiah 23:6)

Jehovah Shamma – "the LORD is there" (Ezekiel 48:35)

Jehovah Elohim Israel – "the LORD God of Israel" (Judges 5:3)

Jehovah Rapha – "the LORD that heals you" (Exodus 15:26)

Qadash Israel – "the Holy One of Israel" (Isaiah 1:14)

SCRIPTURES THAT SPEAK LIFE AND GIVE YOU HOPE

Proverbs 31:30 (NIV): *"Charm is deceptive, and beauty is fleeting;*
but a woman who fears the Lord is to be praised."

Psalm 46:5 (NIV): *"God is within her, she will not fall;*
God will help her at break of day."

Proverbs 31:16-17 (NIV): *"She considers a field and buys it;*
out of her earnings she plants a vineyard.
She sets about her work vigorously;
her arms are strong for her tasks."

1 Corinthians 15:10 (NIV): *"But by the grace of God I am what I am, and his grace to me was not without effect. No, I worked harder than all of them—yet not I, but the grace of God that was with me."*

Proverbs 31:20-21 (NIV): *"She opens her arms to the poor and extends her hands to the needy.*
When it snows, she has no fear for her household;
for all of them are clothed in scarlet."

2 Corinthians 12:9 (GNT): *But his answer was: "My grace is all you need, for my power is greatest when you are weak." I am most happy, then, to be proud of my* weaknesses, in order to feel the protection of Christ's power over me."

Galatians: 5:22-23 (GNT): *"But the Spirit produces love, joy, peace, patience, kindness, goodness, faithfulness, humility, and self-control. There is no law against such things as these."*

Isaiah 41:10 (NIV): *"Do not fear, for I am with you; do not be dismayed, for I am your God. I will strengthen you, I will help you, yes, I will uphold you with My righteous right hand."*

Isaiah 40:3 (NIV): *"...but those who hope in the Lord will renew their strength. They will soar on wings like eagles; they will run and not grow weary, they will walk and not be faint."*

Matthew 6:34 (NIV): *"Therefore do not worry about tomorrow, for tomorrow will worry about itself. Each day has enough trouble of its own."*

Psalm 139:14 (NIV): *"I praise you because I am fearfully and wonderfully made your works are wonderful, I know that full well."*

Joshua 1:9 (NIV): *"Have I not commanded you? Be strong and courageous. Do not be afraid; do not be discouraged, for the Lord your God will be with you wherever you go."*

Psalm 46:1 (NIV): *"God is our refuge and strength, an ever-present help in trouble."*

Luke 1:45 (NIV): *"Blessed is she who has believed that the Lord would fulfill his promises to her!"*

Proverbs 31:25-26 (NIV): *"She is clothed with strength and dignity;*
she can laugh at the days to come. She speaks with wisdom, and faithful instruction is on her tongue."

Proverbs 4:23 (NIV): *"Above all else, guard your heart, for everything you do flows from it."*

Jeremiah 29: 11 (NIV): *"For I know the plans I have for you", declares the Lord, "plans to prosper you and not harm you, plans to give you hope and a future."*

2 Timothy 1:7 (NLT): *"For God has not given us a spirit of fear and timidity, but of power, love, and self-discipline."*

Proverbs 15:1 (NIV): *"The wise woman builds her house, but with her own hands the foolish one tears hers down."*

1 Timothy 3:11 (NIV): *"In the same way, the women are to be worthy of respect, not malicious talkers but temperate and trustworthy in everything."*

Proverbs 31:10-20 (NIV): *"A wife of noble character who can find? She is worth far more than rubies. Her husband has full confidence in her and lacks nothing of value. She brings him good, not harm, all the days of her life. She selects wool and flax and works with eager hands. She is like the merchant ships, bringing her food from afar. She gets up while it is still night; she provides food for her family and portions for her female servants. She considers a field and buys it; out of her earnings she plants a vineyard. She sets about her work vigorously; her arms are strong for her tasks. She sees that her trading is profitable, and her lamp does not go out at night. In her* *hand she holds the distaff and grasps the spindle with her fingers. She opens her arms to the poor and extends her hands to the needy.*"

ABOUT THE AUTHORS

Barbara Johnson is the author of *Alone with God,* and co-author of bestselling book *Warring Women Arise and Pray.* Her goal is to hear God say "well done thou good and faithful servant."

She is Co-Pastor of Yahweh House of Prayer located in Enterprise, Al. Barbara Johnson has a BA degree in Psychology from University of Maryland. She is a Master Cosmetologist, stylist, and owner of Yahweh's Beauty Salon.

Married to Bishop Vernon Johnson for 35 years, they have four sons: Marquintez, Demetrius, Melchisedec, and Isaiah Johnson. She knows how to get God's attention through prayer, praise, and worship. Allow the aroma of God's presence surround each of us by reading her prayers on Hope, Despair, and Deliverance.

Contact Information:

Email: psalms91bj@yahoo.com
Facebook: Barbara Johnson
Facebook: Yahew House of Prayer

Kandi is a 47-year-old stroke survivor, and coauthor of bestselling book *Warring Woman Arise and Pray*. She had a stroke in May of 2019, which completely changed her life and her daughter's. She is a fun, caring person who likes to help people and the world around her become a better place. Her love in supporting others by sharing the importance of forgiveness is her calling.

Teaching others how to be strong and forgiving has allowed her to share God's goodness in many ways. She serves as a Moderator for Broken Wings Brain Injury Empowerment Group, an online brain injury support group, where her daily interactions empower, educate, and inspire those with traumatic brain injury and their caregivers to persevere as they travel their journey of hope and healing.

Contact Information:

Email: allkandi@icloud.com
Facebook: Kandi Layton

Barbara A Williams was born to the late Rev. Ovis and Anne Flournoy in Newark, NJ. She attended schools in the Newark and East Orange School districts. Barbara graduated from Northeastern Bible College in Essex Fells, NJ, earning a BA in Biblical Studies and Elementary Education. An alumna of Montclair State University she earned a Master's Degree in Education with an emphasis on Critical Thinking. Her love for children led her to become a Middle School teacher for the Newark school district.

In 2015, Barbara became a caregiver for her mother who was diagnosed with the onset of dementia. In January 2018, she retired from Newark Public Schools and devoted her time as a full-time caregiver for her mom who passed on December 12th, 2019.

A true prayer warrior studying to be a women's life coach, Barbara has a strong desire to minister to women. A member of Divinity Missionary Baptist Church in East Orange NJ, under the leadership of Dr. Byron E Lennon and First Lady Dr. Margaret Lennon she's a licensed evangelist, and part of the Music and Women's Ministry.

She is married to Minister Noble Williams since July 1989, and has two daughters, Kyla and Tiffany, and 4 beautiful grandchildren.

Contact Information:

Email: nobarwill@yahoo.com
Facebook: Barbara Flournoy-Williams & Author Barbara Williams

Arvinese Reid is a prolific author, pastor, proud mother, grandmother, and dear friend. Arvinese coauthored the #1 bestselling book *Confessions of a Caregiver,* and *Born Again Daughters of Zion.* Born to transmute the world and write books, she spent her first days in Suffern, New York at the Good Samaritan Hospital on November 15, 1971. At an early age, Arvinese has always sought to be resilient to the waves of life. Despite her primitive parents and grungy environment she found her joy in the loving support of her daughter Aaliyah Slaughter. Raising a little girl while accomplishing her greatest feat as a mother who fought with her daughter as she faced a terminal illness.

"Be passionate and purpose will find you," said Aaliyah. Arvinese took Aaliyah's last sentiments and produced a community nonprofit organization in Human Services titled, "Single Moms Making Moves." To be remembered is not her mission, but to change a life will be the legacy Arvinese leaves. As she honors the life of Aaliyah, Arvinese continues to spread her nurturing attitude and hopes as you read this book that you're compelled to undergo transformation and see your best you come into fruition.

Contact Information:

Email: arvinese@gmail.com
Facebook: Author Arvinese Reid

Dr. Tanya L. Moses is a servant-leader seeking God's heart daily. She is a member of Intercessory Prayer Ministry and founder of TM Solutions, a consultant with professional and civic affiliations. She earned a Bachelor of Science degree in Criminal Justice at Grambling State University (LA), and a Bachelor in Theology. She holds a Legal Administration degree from the University of Detroit Mercy, and Master and Doctorate degrees in Organizational Leadership from the University of Phoenix.

She is a retired Law Enforcement officer, the mother of Amelie L. Rousseve, and a member of Zeta Phi Beta Sorority, Inc.

Contact Information:

Email: tlmoses3@gmail.com
Facebook: your www.facebook.com/agsudivas.avon.5

Dawn D. Cotterell, a native of Covington, LA, is the Founder/CEO of Dawn D.W. Cotterell Enterprises, Inc. She belongs to Top Ladies of Distinction, Inc., and The Department of Defense Senior Professional Women's Association. She's a member and Team Lead for the Hospitality Ministry at Grace Church in Dumfries, VA, under the leadership of Bishop Derek Grier. She is a 20-year veteran currently working as a federal government civilian in the field of management, manpower data/cyber workforce management, staffing, IT policy and planning, and performance and program management.

A woman of God, strategist, speaker, mentor, and influencer, she and her grandson Carmelo Reyes are the authors of the best-selling book *iBudget-Budget Coloring Books for Kids*. She is also the author of He Holds *My Hand Daily Journal, and a Dawn2Dusk Emergency Planner and Notebook.*

She is currently enrolled in the Master of Legal Studies program at American University's Washington College of Law. She holds MS in Organizational Management, BS in Human Resource Management, and Associate in Applied Science Management with a Minor in Certified Managers and Human Resource Management. She is the mother of Geovanni and Asiah and a Nana to Carmelo.

Contact Information:

Email: dcotterellenterprises@gmail.com
Facebook: facebook.com/dawn.dee.77

Katina Turner is the mother of two adult children, grandmother, daughter, granddaughter, sister, and friend with an amazing and illuminating spirit. She strives each day to be in alignment with her divine soul's purpose to exemplify, model and share with others her spiritual development journey. Over the years, she has co-created a circle of support and resources for individuals working on personal and professional transformation.

Her years of experience being an educator, facilitator, youth specialist, crisis counselor, and intervention and prevention officer has equipped and positioned her to inspire others to turn life challenges and struggles into amazing testimonies.

Contact Information:

Email: katinaturner02@gmail.com
Facebook: Katina Turner

Helen Newlin is the author of *A Daily Surviving Overcomer*. She is a devoted mother of 3 children, 7 grandchildren along with her dog Missy. She is the creator of the Facebook group, "Women Who Are Daily Surviving Overcomers" where daily inspiration is given. She is an entrepreneur of "Overcomers United", an inspirational apparel and gift line.

She's committed to her ministry, Life Changing International Church as a Praise and Worship Leader. Helen loves to cook and show hospitality to all she serves. She's a 20-year clean witness to let other women know they can overcome anything with Christ!

Contact Information:

Email: overcomers351@gmail.com
Facebook: Author Helen Ann Newlin
Facebook: Women Who Are Daily Surviving Overcomers
Facebook: Overcomers United

Born and raised in Savannah, GA, Chiquita Frazier was born on November 16, 1975. She is a single mother of three amazing kids and two awesome grandkids whom she loves dearly. She attended school with the Savanah Chatham County school systems where she graduated from Jenkins High School in 1995. She earned her first associate degree in Early Childhood Care & Education in 2006. She later went back to complete her bachelor's degree where she received a Bachelor of Arts in Early Childhood Education & Administration in 2013. Lastly, she completed her Master's Degree in Business Administration in 2017.

She has worked in the Chatham country school system for 20 years were she's had the pleasure of working with kids for 15 of the twenty years there. Her current position as an Assistant Asset Manager with the Housing Authority of Savannah allows her to work closely helping people in the community where she has served for the last four years. She is a member of Real life Christian Fellowship Church under the leadership of Pastors Paul and Lesley Taylor. A cancer survivor and a lover of the Lord, she enjoys life even with its up and downs. Trusting and depending on God is an essential part of her life. She's excited to see what God has in store for her future.

Contact Information:

Email: tonya0125@hotmail.com
Facebook: Tonya Love

Dr. Stacy L. Henderson, a native of Savannah, Georgia, is a retired Naval Officer, Christian educator, inspirational speaker, businesswoman and an international best-selling author. She speaks four languages and has publications in more than 40 language translations - with two in the White House Library. Her Stacy's Stocking Stuffers Christmas Charity has provided toys, meals, coats, clothing, and monetary support for families around the world since 1991. She has countless military and civilian accolades.

Stacy is a domestic abuse survivor turned advocate who motivates and inspires others to achieve their best mental, physical and spiritual health. She is a Dean of Christian Leadership Schools at Christ Temple Baptist Church, Markham, Illinois and maintains close ties with her lifelong church family at Little Bryan Baptist Church, Savannah, Georgia. She utilizes her spiritual gifts to glorify God and edify His people.

She is a wife, a mother of two adult children (KeiSha and William), has a daughter-in-love (Mona), and several bonus children and grandchildren - comprising a blessed and beautiful 'Blended and Extended' Family. To God be the Glory!

Contact Information:

Email: Drstacylhenderson@gmail.com
Instagram - @SLHenderson007

Bishop-designate Jackqueline R. Easley is the Senior Pastor of Faith & Love Christian Ministries, where she serves the people of God along with her husband Pastor Marvin E. Easley. Bishop-designate Jackqueline has a blended family which includes 3 sons, one daughter, and eight grandchildren. She is a Nurse Educator at The Department of Veterans Affairs; she holds her Masters in Nursing Education.

Bishop-designate Jackqueline is the founder of JRE Ministries, where her heart's goal is to serve women with low self-esteem, low confidence, and who have lost children to violence. She also is the founder of Shelton Smyles, an organization birthed out of the pain she endured from the loss of her son to violence. She is one of the co-authors of BADZ (Born Again Daughters of Zion), transformational stories of Revelation, Resilience, & Recovery. Her weapon for the enemy is Praise and Prayer.

Contact Information:

Email: flcmpastor1@gmail.com
Facebook: Jackqueline Easley
Instagram: pastorje

Sharon Rayford is an upcoming co-author of *HIS DESTINY HER PURPOSE* while working on some writings of her own. She is a wife, mother, and two times Iraqi Veteran. Trials, tragedy, and pain do not define her. She is a minister and currently attends seminary in the Masters of Divinity program. She enjoys outreach; including visiting nursing homes and prison ministry.

Her outgoing personality merges easily in ministry, being a hairstylist, makeup artist, crafter, and more. She prays that lives will shift from fear to faith. She does not seek a spotlight, but rather shines Christ upon others.

Contact Information:

Email: ministrymissionandmore@gmail.com
Facebook: The-Rayfords Newbeginning

Melquita Singleton was born and raised in Savannah, GA. She was only 4 years old when her father tragically died. Her mom raised her to be a caring, loving, and God-fearing young lady.

She graduated from Savannah High School and Savannah Arts Academy in 1999 with a Major in Dance. After high school she enrolled in The Healthcare Administration Program at The University of Phoenix while working at Memorial Health University. She graduated with a Bachelors of Science in Healthcare Administration. In that same year, she gave birth to her son and five years later welcomed her daughter.

In 2016, she and her children were victims of a hit-and-run which left her in a coma fighting for her life. This was the point she was drawn closer to God than ever before. Today, she can truly say she is thankful to still have life!

Contact Information:

Email: melquitaswinton6399@gmail.com
Facebook: Melquita Singleton

Lineshia Arrick is a fun, energetic young woman who is full of life. She gave her life to Christ at an early age. She was raised by her single mother in Birmingham, AL. Lineshia is the mother of her only son Hezekiah Williams, who passed away in 2009. She earned her associate degree at Virginia College. Her love for medicine and helping others is her daily drive. She has been working in the medical field for eight years.

Caring for her mother for years is what drove her to explore medicine and discovered it was her passion. She instantly fell in love with the thought of being able to help others. In 2015, she and the love of her life Eugene Arrick began dating, and in 2009 they married.

She later lost her inspiration, the trailblazer of her family, her mother. Evolving into everything she wants to be in Christ she enrolled into online Bible courses. Her favorite quote is "Always strive to be the best you, you can be!"

Contact Information:

Email: Hezekiah2.lw@gmail.com
Instagram: figuresandfitness_arrcks

Dawn Pullin, is the visionary of Phenomenal Woman Award Celebration and Phenomenal Woman D.P. Ministries whose goal is to empower women and girls to live in their Phenomenal. She is also the Executive Director of Restoration Community Services LLC; a community based behavioral health and addiction treatment agency.

She received her Bachelors' Degree from Norfolk State University and a Masters of Arts in Education from Malone College. Dawn is a Licensed Professional Counselor, Chemical Dependency Counselor Assistant, and Grief Recovery Method Specialist.

Dawn published the Phenomenal Woman Journal and first book titled, WHILE *WAITING ON GOD TO ANSWER*: How to maintain a posture of expectancy as you wait to hear from God.

Contact Information:

Email: phenomenalwoman11@yahoo.com
Website: phenomenalwoman11.com
Facebook: Dawn Pullin
IG: Dawn Pullin
Twitter: dpullin11

Gilana Pearce is a health educator, group fitness instructor and network marketer who is known as the sister that leaves you greater after every conversation. Gilana's mission is to have real conversations about LIFE from a mental, spiritual and physical standpoint.

As an author, group fitness instructor and nutrition coach, Gilana is an author of two books: *Learning to Initiate Forgiveness in Everything (L.I.F.E) and From Pain to Freedom* A Self-Forgiveness Journal where she outlines simple, realistic steps to a better perspective on life.

Gilana is a food enthusiast who loves to explore new foods and teaches others better choices they would not usually be exposed to eating due to their culture and environment.

Contact Information:

Email: iamgilanapearcetheauthor@gmail.com
Website: www.gilanapearce.com
Facebook: Gilana Pearce

Cynthia Rucker Collins is the founder and CEO of Empowering You Ministries. She attended Winston-Salem Forsyth County Schools and she is pursuing her undergraduate degree at Winston-Salem State University in Interdisciplinary Studies.

She hosts an international radio show, "You Are More Than A Conqueror" and it is aired on the 2nd Tuesday of each month at 8:00 pm EST. She has directed a documentary titled *Ashes to Beauty: From Defeat to a Conqueror*. She is the Ministry Director of "The Sisterhood - A Movement" which is a Christian-based organization. Cynthia is a co-author of *Owning Your Uniqueness Your Voice Matters*.

An evangelist and mentor, she loves ministering to hurting women, because she overcame a toxic relationship. Cynthia is happily married to Roosevelt Collins, and they live in Winston-Salem, NC. She is available for speaking engagements, and you can connect with her via email or her social media platform.

Contact Information:

Email: collinscynthia663@gmail.com
Facebook: Cynthia.rucker.14

Evette Corbin is a dynamic women's ministry leader and Bible teacher. In 2004, she began Faithseed Ministries in her home with a vision to support and equip women in their God-given calling through prayer, teaching, and encouragement.

Evette is a John Maxwell Certified Coach and Trainer. She facilitates training in DISC assessment and leadership principles. She is a retired educator, counselor, and workshop presenter with over thirty years providing guidance and career development to adult students.

Evette and her husband reside in the Bronx, NY, and attend a church where they, along with others, lead a weekly prayer meeting.

Contact Information:

Email: faithseed777@yahoo.com
Website: www.johncmaxwellgroup.com/evettecorbin

A native of Kenya, East Africa, Dr. Anastasia Freeborn is the pastor of Streams in the Desert International Church in Bakersfield, California. A graduate of Living Waters Bible Institute in Pasadena, California, she's an ordained chaplain under Healing Word Ministries. She attended Summit Bible College, Bakersfield, California graduating with a Bachelor of Theology with an emphasis in Christian Leadership. She obtained a Masters in Theology with emphasis in Christian Counseling and completed her Doctorate Degree in Christian Counseling, with a focus in marriage and grief counseling, as well.

She entered the Little Sisters of Saint Francis as an aspirant nun at the age of 16. She also worked for the US Peace Corps Volunteer Services and was later hired by the US Embassy in Nairobi, Kenya as a language and cross-cultural instructor. She has traveled to many countries, including England, Germany, Australia, New Zealand, Russia, and Israel as an evangelist and conference speaker.

An award-winning poet, and author of *Finally, It's Beginning to Rain,* she's the mother of three children, the youngest in high school.

Contact Information:

Email: ukambanifreeborn@gmail.com
Website: seasonedruth.com

Twylia G. Reid obtained a B.S. Degree in Business Administration at Trident University International and is a 20-year US Army disabled retiree.

She is a Best-Selling, Multi-Award-Winning, Multi-Published Non-Fiction Author, 2020 Success Women National Top Influencer Nominee, 2019 Trinity Nonprofit Awards Finalist, 2019 Blacks In Government Featured Speaker, 2019 110th NAACP Conference Featured Author/Panelist Moderator, 2019 Unspoken Wounds Women Veteran's Portrait of Personal Courage Award Recipient, 2019 ACHI (Strength In Sisterhood) Magazine Woman of Achievement & Author of the Year Award Nominee, 2018 48th Congressional Legislative Caucus Featured Author, 2019 Winner of The Authors Show Health/Fitness/Wellness Top Female Author, 2018 Winner of The Authors Show Female Non-Fiction Author, 2017 American Book Fest Best Book Awards Finalist, The Huffington Post Expert Feature Series "Who's Who –10 Black Female Experts to Watch in 2018" selected, and the 2017 Indie Author Legacy Award Author of the Year Finalist.

She is a native of Mississippi who currently resides in Savannah, GA. A self-published author and coach, her ability to take her life's challenges and turn them into books to empower, educate, and enlighten others has allowed her to write content for survivors of traumatic events and their caregivers by teaching them how to create the life they desire in spite of the challenges faced after their tragedy.

She is a woman who truly loves God and loves God's people. She's very passionate about her Christian walk and call into ministry, and grateful for the gift God has entrusted her with, which she uses for the advancement of His Kingdom.

She's the Founder and CEO of ***Broken Wings, Inc.***, a 501(c)3 Nonprofit Organization that provides resources and prevention insight to traumatic brain injury survivors and their families, and the founder of ***Broken Wings Brain Injury Empowerment Group***, an online brain injury support group. She's the Founder and CEO of ***When Heaven Speaks, LLC – Book Coaching & Publishing***, minister, speaker, brain injury community advocate, and the Executive Producer/Host of the ***Conquerors Café*** on Blog Talk Radio, which spotlight authors, entrepreneurs, and survivors who've endured horrific life-changing hardships ready to share their testimonies of hope and healing with the world. She is also the CEO and Founder of ***When Heaven Speaks Learning Academy,*** an online learning space offering the tools and skills needed to learn and implement the steps of developing a positive mindset to become the best you that you can be!

To date, Twylia has authored over 24 titles with the following being Best Sellers: ***"Broken Wings"*** written to help others understand the life of a brain injury survivor and his caregiver's journey through his recovery; ***"What Do You Do…When Caregivers Need Care Given,"*** a resource for those operating in the role as a caregiver to those with chronic or lifelong illnesses; ***"Confessions of a Caregiver"***, a powerful anthology that tells the testimonies of 7 caregivers and how they maintained their faith and perseverance during their caregiving journey; ***"From Tragedy To Working Strategies,"*** a resource guide that teaches survivors strategies to help them turn their traumatic events into empowering moments; *"**Just Because I Have A Brain Injury Doesn't Mean…**"* coauthored with her traumatic brain-injured son, Mylon, highlighting things brain injury survivors want you to know and understand; "**Warring Women Arise and Pray**" an anthology overflowing with heartfelt, and insightful supplications that will promote your communication with God to higher levels; "**Affirmations for the Mind, Body, & Soul**" A Guide for Survivors of Traumatic Events, coauthored by her daughter, NaSharee.

Grateful for the support she's received, and passionate about her role as a traumatic brain injury advocate and caregiver, as the visionary author of this anthology, inspiring and motivating others is what she lives for. Empowering, educating, and enlightening others is her calling. Her mantra is: "Aspiring to Inspire Others"!

Other books she's written: a Christian Coloring Book Series (*Beauty for Ashes*, *Journey to the Sacred Garden*, *Amazing Animals*, and *The Promises of God*), *SOARING By the Power of God: 31-Day Devotional For Spirit Filled Living*, *When Caregivers Need Care Given Daily Journal*, *My Journey Goal Setting Journal*, *The WORD, the Truth & the Light: Bible Study Notebook*, *A Survivor's Goal Planning Journal: A Brain Injury Survivor's Guide to Goal Setting*, *Pray Believe Receive Prayer Journal*, and Monthly Planners

Contact Information:

Email: info@twyliareid.com
Facebook: @authortwyliareid
Facebook: @BWINC
Facebook: @conquerorscafe
Facebook: @whenheavenspeakspublishing
IG/Twitter: @tgreid02
Website: www.twyliareid.con

Website: www.whenheavenspeakspublishing.com
Website: www.conquerorscafe.com
Website: www.brokenwinginc.org

WE WANT TO HEAR FROM YOU

If this book has made a difference in your life,
I would be delighted to hear about it!

Leave a review on Amazon.com

BOOK TWYLIA TO SPEAK AT YOUR NEXT EVENT

Send an email to: **info@twyliareid.com**

Learn more about Twylia and her journey of hope and
healing at:
www.TwyliaReid.com

If you would like to donate to help spread awareness
about traumatic brain injury and the devastation it
causes families,
please visit:

www.brokenwingsinc.org

RECOMMENDED READINGS

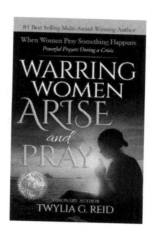

Reid, Twylia G. *WARRING WOMEN ARISE AND PRAY: When Women Pray Something Happens.* Savannah, Georgia: When Heaven Speaks, 2020.

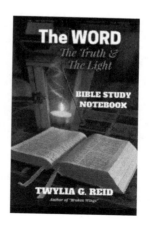

Reid, Twylia G. *The WORD The Truth & The Light: BIBLE STUDY NOTEBOOK.* Savannah, Georgia: Broken Wings, 2018.

Reid, Twylia G. *SOARING By The Power of God: 31 Day Devotional.*
Savannah, Georgia: Broken Wings, 2020.

Reid, Twylia G. *Affirmations For the Mind, Body & Soul: A Guide for Survivors of Traumatic Events.* Savannah, Georgia: Broken Wings, 2018.

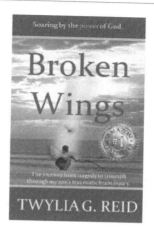

Reid, Twylia G. ***Broken Wings.*** Savannah, Georgia: Savannah, Georgia: Broken Wings, 2020.

Reid, Twylia G. ***From Tragedy To Working Strategies.*** Savannah, Georgia: Savannah, Georgia: Broken Wings, 2020.

Reid, Twylia G. *What Do You Do…When Caregivers Need Care Given. Caring For Yourself While Caring For Others.* Savannah, Georgia: Broken Wings, 2018.

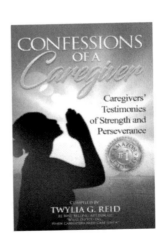

Reid, Twylia G. *CONFESSIONS OF A CAREGIVER Caregivers' Testimonies of Strength and Perseverance.* Savannah, Georgia: When Heaven Speaks, 2019.

HIS DESTINY...HER PURPOSE

(Matters of the Heart)

HABITS OF A GODLY WOMAN

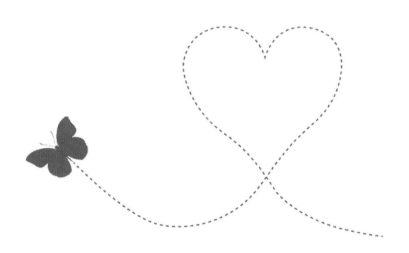

www.WhenHeavenSpeaksPublishing.com